Million Dollar Ebay Business From Home

A Step-by-Step Guide

Neil Waterhouse

Published by:
21st Generation Publishing
4747 36th Street
Suite 9956
Long Island City
New York 11101
Phone: 888 611 1260
Fax: 888 611 2566
Email: info@21stGenerationPublishing.com

eBay™ is a registered trademark of eBay Inc.

Warning/Disclaimer

This book is designed to provide information on building an eBay/e-commerce business. It is sold with the understanding that the publisher and author are not engaged in rendering legal, accounting, or other professional services. If legal or other expert assistance is required, the services of a competent professional should be sought.

It is not the purpose of this book to reprint all of the information that is otherwise available to authors and publishers, but instead to complement, amplify, and supplement other texts. You are urged to read all of the available material, learn as much as possible, and tailor the information to your own individual needs.

Every effort has been made to make this book as complete and as accurate as possible, but there may be errors, both typographical and in content. Therefore, the text should be used only as a general guide, and not as the ultimate source of information. Furthermore, this book contains information that is current up to the printing date.

The purpose of this book is to educate and entertain. The author and publisher accept neither a liability nor responsibility to any person or entity with respect to any loss or damage caused, or alleged to have been caused, directly or indirectly, by the information contained in this book. If you do not wish to be bound by the information above, you may return this book to the publisher for a full refund.

*"All our dreams can come true,
if we have the courage to pursue them."*

~ W ALT D ISNEY ~

About the Author

Neil Waterhouse is a pioneer in the computer/e-commerce world. Right from school, he was the first in his high school to have a computer at home. Back in 1980 when the school he attended, Manly Boys High, in Sydney, Australia, received their first computer he was there, teaching his "teachers" how to use the computer. From there, he had his first part-time job demonstrating Apple computers at Sydney's Royal Easter Show, when he was just 15-years-old.

Neil has always worked in the cutting edge of the computer industry, and was one of the first to not only adopt the Internet, but own one of the first Internet service providers in Australia. In 1991, Neil started Cam1 Computer Wholesale, which became one of the largest computer hardware suppliers in Sydney. Neil was also one of the pioneers in implementing Internet marketing, and one of the first to generate over 1 million dollars in sales from home.

Neil started with eBay in 2002, and has sold millions of dollars of items through eBay from his home in Sydney, Australia. In 2009 he was recognized as one of the top eBay sellers, and was invited by eBay to speak on the eBay Top Rated Seller Panel. Neil is also the founder of Waterhouse Research, which is the world's largest research company that specializes in finding high-profit products for eBay and online businesses.

Neil not only runs multiple eBay businesses - he studies the eBay and e-commerce industry. He doesn't just talk about the industry - he teaches it.

Neil shows people how to make a difference while making a living from home. His mission is to assist as many people as possible with learning how to make a living from home.

Table of Contents

Introduction

My goal for this book is to give a step-by-step guide so the reader can duplicate the steps we use for our million dollar eBay home business. Included in the book are all the tools required for building an eBay business of any size you wish, whether you're a mother looking to earn enough money from home so that you do not have to go back to work, or an entrepreneur who wishes to build a multimillion dollar eBay business. Either way, we are all so lucky that eBay and the Internet have given us this platform whereby we can work from home. eBay has the ability to provide an amazing lifestyle and only the size of your dreams limit the size of your eBay businesses.

If you can use the Internet, you have all that it takes to own an eBay business. It doesn't matter if you only have two cents in the bank, either. I will show you how my wife, Nicole, and I, as well as many of my students, have started our eBay businesses without spending one cent.

Changes

Like the world, eBay is continually changing. You may see some screenshots in this book which differ from the eBay images online.

Feedback

I love to hear any feedback or questions you may have. Please email me at neil@neilwaterhouse.com I always make the effort to read every email.

Please also check my blog at www.neilwaterhouse.com for answers to frequently asked questions.

CHAPTER ONE

Why eBay?

"The secret of getting ahead is getting started."

~ SALLY BERGER ~

I, like many, vastly underestimated the power of the eBay platform.
I say to all of my students:
"DO NOT UNDERESTIMATE the eBay opportunity."
Let me show you why we chose eBay over the many other types
of businesses available.

Back in 2000, I sold my computer business, and finding a new
cash cow became my obsession. After being in the computer industry for 19 years, I was bored of getting up early, getting dressed up,
driving to work, working all day, and then driving back home in
the early evening. I wanted a change and I wanted to work from
home.

From 2000, I tested business after business, trying to find
which one made the most money and suited the home Internet

lifestyle the best. By the word *testing* I mean getting my hands dirty by starting and actually running each different type of business. I share this quick overview with you of some of the businesses so you can hopefully save yourself from wasting years of time and over a million dollars.

"Hindsight is a double-edged sword. Too much of it and the past seems inevitable, with too little hindsight, a panoramic perspective is impossible."

~ LANCE B. KURKE: THE WISDOM OF ALEXANDER THE GREAT ~

In 2000, after selling my computer business, CAM1 Computer Wholesale, finding the simplest and most profitable home business became my obsession. I just wanted a simple business which produced enough cash to allow my wife, Nicole, and I to work from home; therefore enabling us to spend more time with our children, as well as providing enough spare cash - and spare time – to pursue the other things we enjoy in life: traveling, hobbies, etc.

Searching for the most profitable home business took me all over the world to meet the people who are at the top of their game, including meeting the second richest man in the world, Warren Buffet, in his home town of Omaha, Nebraska, USA. (More about that meeting shortly).

My goal was to hunt down the fastest and most profitable ways to make money from home.

During testing, we call the best performing business our "control business," and we are always looking to better it. If new businesses outperform our control business, they then become the new control business.

Sometimes in this book, I may show you something which could be perceived as "showing off." This is not my intention. What I am about to reveal to you is not done to "wave my own flag" or to "show off."

My aim is to show you the evidence behind the extensive research and testing my staff and I have carried out, in order to demonstrate how good the eBay opportunity is compared with other business opportunities we have tested. Over the last decade, the options of working from home have improved dramatically. This is thanks to the Internet, mainly, as it gives us the ability to access 6,930,055,154 (nearly 7 billion) Internet users worldwide - from our couches in our living rooms - and that figure is growing every day.

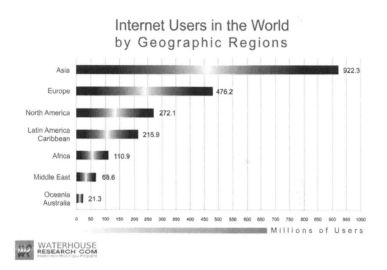

Internet Users in the World by Geographic Regions

Even better news: You no longer need any money or a ton of time to make money from home. However, according to the latest data, most people are going in the wrong direction.

The current buzz is social media. Millions of people are using social media sites like Facebook and Twitter, etc., to build social media businesses, which is massively time-consuming. However, the latest data (below) shows that social media is not where the money is, with only 4% of the money being spent on the Internet going to social media. In addition, this 4% has massive competition from everybody trying to make a dollar on the social media platforms.

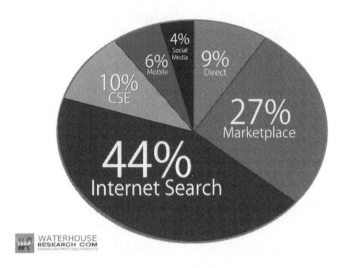

We need our home businesses to be in the most profitable area with the least competition.

The "Pareto principle" (also known as the 80-20 rule) states that 80% of the effects come from 20% of the causes. What that means to you and I is that 80% of the profits come from only 20% of what we do. The secret is to work out exactly what makes the most money for the least amount of effort, and then do more of it. This 80/20 rule is used by almost all highly successful business people. If you would like to know more about the 80/20 principle, I highly recommend David Koch's *The 80/20 Principle*.

From the graph above, only 4% of e-commerce (Internet sales) is done through social media, and that 4% is mostly from big retailers like Victoria's Secret, as you can see from the chart below.

Top Facebook Fan Pages

Rank	Retailer	Fans
1	Victoria's Secret	19,132,749
2	Walmart	18,017,367
3	Target	16,037,253
4	Adidas Originals	15,128,498
5	Burberry	13,106,495
6	Levi's	12,979,411
7	Victoria's Secret Pink	12,061,108
8	Lacoste	10,031,286
9	WWE	9,617,588
10	Nike	9,767,448
11	Hollister Co.	8,988,903
12	Gucci	8,712,766
13	Aeropostale	7,644,351
14	Kohl's	7,494,084
15	Forever 21	7,192,538
16	Abercrombie & Fitch	6,823,710
17	American Eagle Outfitters	6,764,682
18	NFL	6,009,338
19	Best Buy	6,086,978
20	Dolce & Gabbana	5,625,454
21	Ralph Lauren	5,092,973
22	Hot Topic	4,610,463
23	Old Navy	4,340,147
24	Coach	3,570,223
25	Game&top	2,085,222

WATERHOUSE
RESEARCH.COM
FINDING HIGH PROFIT EBAY PRODUCTS

Just so we are speaking the same language, let's confirm exactly what a home businesses is.

When push comes to shove, some people are looking for a business from which money flows into their bank account for doing nothing or selling nothing. Let's be honest, when was the last time you sent money to someone else's business in exchange for them doing nothing or supplying nothing?

We cannot do 'nothing' and get paid for it, but we can be very smart in what we are willing to do - and critically, *not* do - to get people to send us money. This forms a huge part of the criteria for a home business, tailored to your needs.

We all differ in terms of values, likes and dislikes. Some people love selling: I hate it, and would prefer to spend time with my children. I urge you to write criteria of what you are willing to do and - most importantly - *not* do.

This is my latest criteria for a home business, but it was not this specific back in 2000, when I started researching home businesses. I had to learn the hard way with my own time and money.

- No ceiling limit to the maximum amount you can earn.
- No MLM (Multi-Level Marketing).
- Must be fun: We only get one life; lets' enjoy it.
- Must be family-friendly: I have four children and I like getting them involved.
- Must be simple: This is a lesson from the business investor, Warren Buffet (again, the second richest man in the world). Warren only gets involved in basic businesses which he understands. A home business must be very simple, too. In our experience, if you cannot explain it in one paragraph, to a ten-year-old, then it is too complex.
- Location: My wife, Nicole, grew up on 100 acres in Canada and has always had a yearning to live on a farm again, so it was even more critical for us to have businesses which can be run from a remote location.
- No affiliate marketing.

Affiliate marketing was very profitable years ago, however, Google has pretty much banned it now. If you don't know what you are doing with affiliate marketing, then it is a good way to suck your credit card dry very quickly, and also get banned from ever advertising with Google again.

No writing and selling e-books! I have written and sold many e-books and had some good successes. One website selling an e-book of mine joined Alexa's Top 20,000 Most-Visited Sites on the Planet: That e-book sold over one million dollars in its first 12 months. However, continually writing e-books is hard work and only fun if you are writing about something you are passionate about.

I wrote a course on how to do it back in 2006; however, the strategy we use to make money on eBay today is much simpler.

- No social media: Social media involves spending endless hours creating social media sites, collecting a zillion followers. We are not interested in having a zillion friends on Facebook. All we want is the maximum profit for the least amount of time and money.
- Highly automated: Must be able to run by itself, 24/7.
- Must have a diverse product portfolio for stability: I call this the Natural Tree theory. Let me explain . . .

In nature, each separate leaf of a tree captures sunlight; the more leaves or leaf area a tree has the more sunlight it captures. If one leaf falls off, it is no matter, as there are many more.

Following nature, a strong stable business also looks like a tree with many leaves on it, but in a good eBay business, instead of capturing sunlight, every leaf is another low cost, high profit product.

"I mean if you put all of your eggs in one basket, boy, and that thing blows up you've got a real problem."

~ JERRY BRUCKHEIMER ~

Taking this lesson from nature provides us a very stable, diverse business with many different income streams flowing into your bank account.

Lifestyle

This, for me, is the most important criteria. We only get one chance at life: It is critical we try our best to enjoy every second of it.

Long ago, I realized that when most people are lying on their deathbed, about to pass away, they do not wish they had spent more time at work. They wish they had spent more quality time with their family.

97% of people who own their own business really just have a job, but they will rarely admit it. They spend more hours working in their own business and get paid less than they would if they had a conventional job.

The best home businesses provide multiple money streams, protecting you from market changes and thus giving you a good nights sleep.

- Recession proof: In hard times, people stop buying houses, cars, boats, holidays, etc., but they still buy small things to make them happy. Despite world recessions, e-commerce continues to grow at double-digit rates.
- No fads.
- Non-seasonal.

To know why we chose eBay out of all the other home businesses out there, it is critical I share with you how we got there.

Back in 1991, I started a part-time computer company in the spare room of our house and called it CAM1 Computer Wholesale. This part-time business sold computers and peripherals. On Saturday mornings, I would drive over to the other side of the city to pick up parts from an importer, then come home and screw the computers together.

I would then run a small advertisement in the paper and sell the computers during the week to people who would come over to the house and pick them up at night, or after work, or on the weekends.

At first, I screwed together one computer per week, then two, three, four . . . after six months, it had grown to over 20 computers per week. At that point, I made the jump to being full-time and the business grew and grew; then it changed tack and I started receiving orders from companies as well as individuals.

Supplying companies seemed great as it was all done over the phone, by fax, and through couriers; very rarely ever meeting with people. (Not having to talk to people would later become part of my criteria for the perfect home business).

It got to the point where the house and garage were bursting at the seams. It was time to spend some money and lease office space. All of sudden, I realized I had lost the luxury of working from home in my favorite tracksuit, along with the other luxuries of working from home.

Now, with the external office, I had to get up earlier to get dressed, and then waste more time driving to the office. I really missed the luxuries of working from home. I promised myself the next business would be home-based.

CAM1 grew and grew. By the year 2000, it had 18 staff and consumed my life. Often, I would start at seven a.m. and get home 12-plus hours later. It was killing me, and my family life: time to sell... and I sold it at the end of 2000.

The Good, the Bad, and the Ugly Lessons from CAM1

The Good:
- Strong cash flow.
- Reasonably good profits.

The Bad:
- High capital, with over half a million dollars invested borrowed.
- Had to be at the office to make sure it ran correctly, thereby dramatically affecting lifestyle.

Next Business

My dad got me into computers, but it was never my passion. When I was 15-years-old, he took me to his beloved Apple Users group. By the end of the meeting, two ladies who owned a relatively new computer store called "The Computer Shop" stood up and asked if someone could demonstrate the new Apple II computer at the upcoming Easter show. Suddenly, my arm was in the air, mainly thanks to my dad. Two weeks later, during the school holidays, I had my first part-time computer job demonstrating Apple II computers.

I tried explaining to everybody that my knowledge and desires were purely in how to load Pac-Man and other games from the tape into the computer. Back in those days, that was apparently enough background to demonstrate a computer.

After leaving school, I worked full-time for the Computer Shop, never really enjoying it as it was not my passion; but, like many people, as I got older and accrued more life expenses, I found myself in the position of being locked into the industry I knew, as I could make more money from it than anything else.

With the sale of CAM1 19 years later, I was fortunate to have some spare cash so I could finally, after 19 years, break away from the computer industry. Time to do something for fun!

At the time, cars were my passion. From 1997, to test the market, I began importing a few cars, part-time, into Australia from Japan and the USA, and even sold some to celebrities like Rene Rivkin, who purchased a Dodge Viper that I had imported from the USA and converted to right-hand drive.

Again, I do not show pictures like this to wave my own flag or show off; they are there purely because a picture speaks a thousand words.

For the Vipers, I had set up another business called Cam 1 Conversions. The Vipers had to be converted from left-to right-hand drive, which was a pretty big job. It took 18 months for the Government to approve the conversion and to issue us with a license that allowed us to convert 25 per year.

In 2002, two years after the sale of the computer company, I suddenly realized I had leased a workshop and had staff and was again spending increasingly more time at the workshop, away from home. *Déjà vu* all over again. Time to sell the car import business, so in mid-2002 it was also sold.

The Good, the Bad, and the Ugly Lessons from CAM1 Conversions

The Good:
- Good profit when the cars finally sold.

The Bad:
- High capital costs to purchase and hold vehicles.
- Waiting for next sale: Selling big-ticket items demands nerves of steel - very exciting when you get a new sale, then what seems like an eternity until the next one. Very hard to predict cash flow.

2002

After selling the car business, I took 12 months off and started attending seminar after seminar discovering all different ways to make money from home. From Forex trading, options trading, share trading, and even real estate trading to the emerging Internet and eBay.

I did a load of option trading courses and decided to give it a go, full-time. Yep: had a few successes, but the losses were almost always far larger. Later on, I realized my mentor only averaged seven option trades per year, and only when everything lined up perfectly. This bit was left out of the course material!

Warren Buffet, who made his money from investing in existing companies, never, ever sells his shares unless something (negatively) dramatic happens to the company in which he owns shares. As Warren says: "Why sell shares in a good company?"

The Good, the Bad, and the Ugly Lessons from Trading Options and Shares

The Good:
- Can work from home.

The Bad:
- Very scary. Only trade with money you can afford to lose.
- Requires very close monitoring.
- 50% of the market thinks the market will go up.
- 50% of the market thinks it will go down.
- Definitely not idiot-proof.

2003

While running the earlier car business, I had made many trips to Japan to attend car auctions and noticed the huge amount of drink vending machines all over Japan. They were literally everywhere, on almost every street corner: selling cold drinks, hot drinks, food, and even alcohol in public places.

The first time I saw an alcohol vending machine I asked the Japanese associate I was with how this was okay, and why all the kids were not lying on the footpaths in a drunken stupor?

I will never forget his reply: "The kids are told they are not allowed to drink alcohol." *Wow, that stopped them!? What am I doing wrong with my kids!?* I asked myself. I guess in a country where everybody rides their bicycle to the train station, parks it with NO lock, and comes back at night to find it in the same position, anything is possible!

The most popular vending machines in Japan, at the time, held 16 types of drinks: 12 cold, with 4 sections that could be heated up for canned coffee, tea, soup, etc. These machines cost around $13,000 USD each (new), but they could be purchased used for around $4,000 each.

I purchased 20 of them and brought them back to Australia where I had them re-sprayed and refitted with an Australian coin mechanism. The total cost for each machine was just over 5K each. I then started a new company called National Vending Corporation. As soon as the first machine was ready, I employed a sales rep to go out and find sites for the machines.

My sales rep would walk around industrial areas and into businesses, offering them free installation of free-to-use drink vending machines for their warehouses. The only charge was when each time someone purchased a drink. This was good for the management, as the staff did not leave to walk to the local shops and good for us, as we made money every time a drink was sold.

My theory was that these machines were much better than Coca Cola's machines, as we could offer up to 30 varieties of drink. This proved to be a winner, for a while. I kept buying more machines, and 12 months later I had 114 of them, and a nice, big, bank overdraft.

Each machine averaged around $150 revenue per week and some made over $400 per week, with nearly 200% profit. Sounds nice, but there were behind-the-scenes expenses: commissions for the sales rep, two trucks to fill the machines, and two drivers.

The strategy was to continually move the worst-performing machine from the least-profitable location to a new, hopefully better location, thus continually increasing the revenue.

This business was pretty good and could run without me for extended periods, however more and more, people were copying and importing these same machines. Today, they are everywhere.

When my first wife and I decided to go our separate ways, it was time to start selling everything.

2004 – Game Changer

"When one door closes another one opens."

~ ALEXANDER GRAHAM BELL ~

In 2004, I got an offer I could not refuse, and sold National Vending Corporation.

The Good, the Bad, and the Ugly Lessons from Drink Vending Machines

Pros:
- Good cash flow and profit at the beginning, when competition was low.
- Enjoyable lifestyle.

Cons:
- Too easy for the competition to copy.

One of my mentors for shares and real estate was Peter Spann. Peter's claim to fame was that he went from being bankrupt to becoming a multi-millionaire by purchasing houses, condos and apartments, giving them a quick makeover, and then selling them for a profit. Peter did this over 100 times, and in seven years he became a multi-millionaire.

One day, Peter announced he was creating a "platinum" group which would only be available for people who met a certain criteria. Each applicant would be thoroughly screened to make sure that everything they reported in the application was true and correct. There was also a $38,000 annual fee to join the group.

Part of the criteria was as follows:

- Must have a net worth greater than one million dollars. In fact, many of the applicants were multi-millionaires - some even had more money than Peter.
- Must be self-made millionaires: Applicants were not allowed to win it, marry it, or inherit it.
- Must be self-employed.
- Must add something unique to the group so that each member shares exclusive knowledge.
- Must attend every meeting.
- Each meeting would be held somewhere on the planet, and members were only given one month's notice of location. If a member missed a meeting, he or she was dismissed from the group with no refund. As Peter would like to say: "The only excuse for not turning up is a death certificate, to be signed by you and presented by yourself!"

Although very expensive, this group of 105 self-made-millionaires and multi-millionaires seemed like a brilliant place to learn more secrets and collect more ideas for the perfect home business. In June 2004 I received an acceptance letter from Peter.

In addition to learning how each member made their money, we would also study other highly successful people and meet with them in person, including Warren Buffet.

Peter accepted my application into Platinum as I had been doing what I called the "triple-splitter" strategy. That is, you buy an old house on a largish block, subdivide the land, and then build a duplex in the backyard while renovating the original house. (I won't go into this strategy now, as this is more of a wealth-creation strategy than a cash-creating home business. In order to do property developing, you need a good cash flow first, which is what this book is about).

Through Platinum, I learned a lot about the difference between cash flow and wealth. For instance, people often confuse wealth and cash flow. Wealth is our net worth: assets minus liabilities. "Cash flow" provides the income. For lifestyle, we need a good income.

Many of us have a life, however without the style. By that, I mean many people have become millionaires and multi-millionaires due to the last property boom, but have very low cash flow with which to enjoy life (i.e., asset-rich but cash-poor). Cash flow allows us to enjoy life. It enables us to do what we want to do (e.g., Vanuatu, tomorrow!).

Of course, the other thing we need is time. The wealthy are very rarely paid by the hour. The big problem with being paid by the hour is that we can only work so many hours a week, and even doctors who charge $200 per hour have a capped wage (capped by the amount of hours they can work each week).

Surprisingly, out of 105 millionaires in Platinum, not one of them had a cash generating business which met my criteria.

I stayed with the group for two years until I finally found what I had been looking for: The Internet – *the promises and the promises and* ...

2005

2005 was one of the best years of my life... I met my lovely wife, Nicole, and made my first dollar on the Internet from *something costing nothing*. Just like playing golf, that one good shot makes you want to come back for more. That first dollar earned on the net was my first taste of bigger and better things.

Before 2005, the world was awash with hundreds, if not thousands, of different MLM (multi-level marketing) businesses, and many saw this as the best home business option, however, if they had studied the research out there, they would have discovered that the chance of making just an award-wage with MLM is less than .001%.

By 2005, entrepreneurs were quickly switching their attention to the Internet. The promise of sitting on a beach with blue water lapping at their feet, surrounded by palm trees, while consumers deposit money into their bank accounts 24/7, 365 days a year was too good *not* to get involved. Must admit, this sounded pretty good to me, too, so off I went, attending seminar after seminar and reading book after book. In fact, Nicole and I were attending a Dan Kennedy and Perry Marshall seminar in Chicago when she got her first bout of morning sickness and discovered she was pregnant with our first baby girl.

In addition to attending seminars and reading books, I always tried to get some one-on-one time with the speakers to compare notes. (This is where you get the gems of knowledge and not just the hype).

Internet marketer, Derek Gehl.

Legendary business philosopher Jim Rohn, and Dan Kennedy
(who I believe is the best marketer alive today).

Internet marketing guru, Yanik Silver.

I am not telling you this or showing you the pictures to wave my own flag: I am doing this to try to give you an idea of exactly how much research it has taken to understand why we prefer eBay to any other business we have tested, and to hopefully save you a lot of time and money.

My first real proof that there was serious money in Internet marketing was when I got a call from my accountant to schedule a meeting with one of my clients, Dr. Robert Rawson, who was making a fortune on the Internet. Before this, I always wondered if the only person making money was the guy standing on stage, flogging a course. (It turned out that this was very often the case, however, Dr Rawson was doing it for real).

Dr. Robert Rawson

I met up with Robert at Bondi Beach, Sydney, for lunch, and he generously shared with me what he was doing. In turn, I shared what I had learned from all the courses I had attended and the literature I had read. I went home, closed the doors, and began writing sales letters and e-books (i.e., downloadable books).

Six weeks previously, Niq (my wife's nickname) and I had booked a trip to Hong Kong, so I had a deadline to finish my first eBook before departure. I finished it by Friday; we flew out on Saturday.

I will never forget when we got to our hotel in Hong Kong. I logged on to the net and there were $243 of sales: not enough to retire on, but it was a start! I wrote more and more e-books after this, and the revenue grew and grew, but I was beginning to dislike the long hours it took to write e-books.

Each e-book had its own website. Some sites were better than others, and as mentioned above, one even made it into the Top 20,000 Most Visited Sites on the Planet in 2007 (according to Web Information analysts, Alexa). Because of this, I was invited to join Perry Marshall's Roundtable, which I thought would be useful in order to see what others were doing on the net.

2006

Perry is known as the world's number one go-to guy for advertising with Google. Perry's roundtable members are some of the sharpest Internet marketers on the planet - a great place to get great ideas, and to sound new ones to the group.

There is at least one person in the group who spends over one million dollars per month with Google AdWords. Like Peter Spann's group, there are guidelines to become a member (as well as the $10,000 per year membership fee, plus another 10k, plus travel).

I'm the ugly one on the far left in the striped shirt,
sitting next toPerry, at a meeting in Florida.

Back when I first joined Perry's group, in 2006, we were spending
around $80,000 USD per month on Google AdWords.

Here is a screenshot of our Google account:

The strategy then was to spend one dollar on Google, buying
traffic, and receive two dollars back by selling something that cost
zero dollars (e.g., an e-book). The other part of the strategy was
to continually write more e-books, however, continually writing
e-books is hard work. There must be an easier way?
Back in those days there were two main ways to make money on
the net:

1. Sell a product: either a physical product, like a plant pot,
   or a digital product, like an e-book (downloadable book).
2. Affiliate Marketing (i.e., sell someone else's product).

2007 – "Bait and Switch" Scam: Affiliate Advertising

2007 became the year of the "Google slaps," that is, Google started banning sites that did not have "unique information." Affiliate sites do not meet Google's criteria, as they sell other people's products, and, therefore, are not unique.

Many people had their businesses wiped out literally overnight. I still remember exactly where I was standing when I first heard about the Google slaps, and how many people's businesses had been wiped out. I quickly logged into my Google accounts to see if we had copped it, too.

Fortunately, all of our sites were our own creation, and the slap did not affect us. In fact, it helped us, as it removed a lot of competition.

As affiliates could no longer buy traffic from Google, they had to find a new way to get traffic to their affiliate websites (which sold other people's products). Someone out there had figured out that to get a lot of traffic, all you need to do is find a person or product which gets high traffic and write something like: "Is this item/person a scam? Read this first."

Of course, curiosity gets the cat, and people click this "bait and switch" ad (taking the bait), and are normally fed some story about why the product that a certain company sells is more popular (the switch).

This bait and switch technique is incredibly effective; however, I do not endorse this type of unethical behavior in any form. Thankfully, Google is slowly but surely shutting these sites down.

The popular "Rich Jerk" work-from-home program got nailed first by this strategy. Many companies would create an ad with phrases such as: "Rich Jerk is a scam. Read this first."

It did not matter which niche you were in: the affiliate marketers had software to find all of the high-traffic sites.

For example, one of my sites, www.allaboutfishing.com, was hit (which was literally all about fishing), and it attracted over 30 bait-and-switch affiliate marketers.

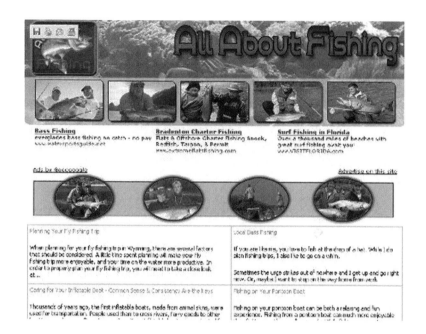

Another site was called Waterhouse Report, which was originally a monthly email about the home business ideas that I had discovered each month. I used to email a basic report to friends and associates, for free, every month, in return for any new information they had come across.

One day, one of my associates rang me and said, "We are going to have another baby and need more money. When's the next Waterhouse Report coming?" and that is how the name Waterhouse Report came to be.

I launched the Waterhouse Report in 2006, and it became quite a hit, with several thousand visitors a day. This, sure enough, grabbed the attention of the bait and switch affiliate marketers.

The Good, the Bad, and the Ugly Lessons from Internet Marketing

Pros:
- Good cash flow, low cost.
- Satisfactory lifestyle (however, you need to continually write new e-books).

Cons:
- Easy to steal.
- Must keep creating new products.

eBay

Niq and I had been buying and selling things on eBay since 2002 and had reasonable success. By 2005, it was time to up the ante. I purchased every eBay book I could get my hands on and signed up for every eBay seminar I could find, and sales quickly started to grow.

My goal had always been to run the business from home: to resist the temptation to get an office away from home, and away from my family. For this reason, the goal was to maximize profits from home. My eBay businesses grew and grew. Then, before I knew it, we had a million dollar business and were asked by eBay to speak on a Top Rated seller panel.

eBay Top Rated Seller Panel

Online sales only really started in 1995, when French-born Iranian computer programmer, Pierre Omidyar, started the website AuctionWeb, which was later re-named to eBay. Online sales only really started taking off in 2000, and by 2010, online sales caught up with offline sales.

That is only 10 years for online sales to catch up, and to truly overtake traditional sales, from traditional bricks and mortar stores which have been around since the dawn of time. Every month, traditional retail businesses lose more and more market share as more and more people all over the planet purchase their goods over the Internet.

Today, people are using department stores as product showrooms to touch and feel products before they use the Internet to purchase the item online. Apps, like eBay's Red Laser app, enable us to walk into a shop, scan the barcode of an item with our smartphone, and retrieve the cheapest place to buy the identical item. The bricks and mortar retailers have called this "Scan and Scram!"

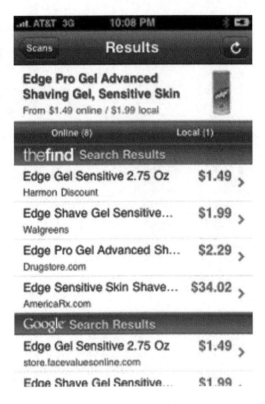

Here in Australia, I have the radio on quietly in the background of my office, and I continually hear a whole gamut of excuses from traditional retailers as to why retail sales have dropped again. Yesterday, they were blaming the new carbon tax which Australia has implemented. Last month, it was wet weather.

The reality is, it is just so much more convenient to order over the Internet, as you almost always find what you want in stock, AND it's usually cheaper, AND it gets delivered to your door!

One of the most fundamental forces changing how people purchase is the smartphone. eBay launched their iPhone application in 2009. In its first year, it did more than $600 million in volume. In 2010, it did $1.75 billion. eBay predicts that over 50% of eBay sales will be done in the future using this app.

More than 35 million people have downloaded eBay's iPhone app at the time of press — it is by far the largest m-commerce application in the world. (M-commerce, or mobile commerce, is the latest new Internet buzz word, meaning "customer purchasing an item from a smart phone"). Mobile devices like smartphones and tablets brings the internet to us seven days a week, 24 hours a day, on our time, at our convenience, where you want to be.

Surveys are now finding out how people shop. People standing in a line at Starbucks can start browsing on eBay.

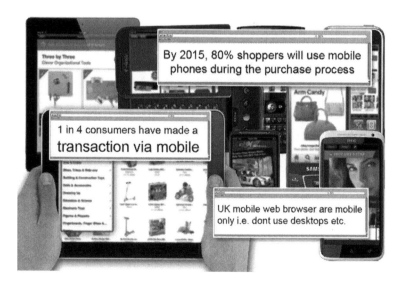

They see something they want, and they buy it, right then and there. Surveys even show that people buy while on the toilet!

Every business on the planet sells either a product or a service. If a business wishes to get an app made, tested and marketed for a smart phone, the average cost is $100,000 USD, and it takes, on average, 18 months to develop, test, and secure Apple's approval.

eBay has spent a lot more than 100k on their app and we all get to use it for free. Thank you eBay!

We can see e-commerce is growing strong at over 10%, while traditional retail is running at minus 3%:

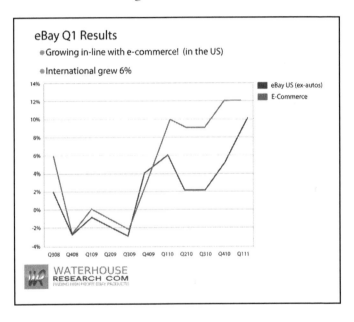

Here is a similar trend from Europe:

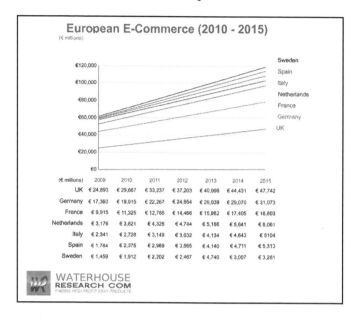

This graph shows similar growth in the UK and Europe:

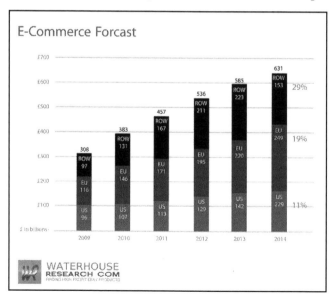

Again, another graph from the U.S. Department of Commerce, J.P. Morgan, Forrester Research, IDC, eMarketer, UK eStats, and TIA with data sources, showing similar high growth in e-commerce:

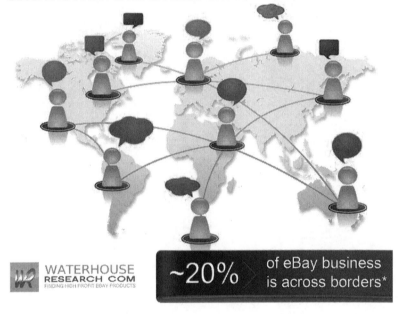

GLOBAL MARKETPLACE ENABLES CROSS-BORDER TRADE

WATERHOUSE RESEARCH COM
FINDING HIGH PROFIT EBAY PRODUCTS

~20% of eBay business is across borders*

eBay reports that 20% of eBay sales are now across borders, allowing us to sell all over the world from our living rooms. Our data shows very similar figures.

In Summary: Why eBay?

- Zero entry cost.
- Access to over 200 million customers worldwide, from your couch.
- Work from home.
- Flexible hours.
- Can grow to any size.

- Unlimited products available.
- Unlimited income potential.
- Easy to automate, so it runs without you.
- Run from anywhere in the world where there is an Internet connection.
- E-commerce is the largest growth market on the planet.
- No royalties or franchise fees.
- Easy to double/quadruple sales by listing exactly the same items on Amazon and your own website. More of this later on.
- No high-capital risk, such as remodelling franchises or shopfronts.
- Low running cost.
- No rent/lease.
- It is your own business: you have no boss looking over your shoulder.
- Huge tax benefits from running a business from home.
- An eBay business is an asset which can be sold or passed on.
- Unlike a traditional bricks and mortar business, an eBay business can be built part-time while you have another job.
- Can be started now!

CHAPTER TWO

What Does a Million Dollar eBay Business Look Like?

"Excess on occasion is exhilarating. It prevents moderation from acquiring the deadening effect of a habit."

~ W. SOMERSET MAUGHAM (THE SUMMING UP, 1938) ~

Let's keep it simple, which it really is. Remember the tree? A strong eBay business looks just like a tree, in which each leaf is a low cost, high-profit product, and every branch is in a different niche.

An example of different niches could be:

- Garden products.
- Bathroom accessories.
- Sewing accessories.
- Bicycle accessories.
- Motor vehicle accessories.

Etc., etc., etc. There are literally hundreds, if not thousands, of different niches. (I will show you more about niches in Chapter 3: What to Sell).

An eBay business, which has many products in many different niches, is protected against any new competitor who is entering the market in a specific niche.

The WORST eBay business is an eBay business that specializes in one niche; has a small amount of different products; and/or has expensive products. If something happens to the niches - like a new aggressive competitor entering the market - your profit could drop on some of the products.

This is not the end of the world, however, as I am going to show you how to buy the products at a cheap price, so there is plenty of profit margin, should this ever happen.

The more leaves (products) your business has, the more money flows into your bank account, making your business more resilient to market fluctuations.

There are three variables which affect how much profit each product makes (based on new products, when you have multiples of the same items):

1. What is the average selling price of the product?
2. How much profit does this product make every time it sells?
3. How many times does each product sell per month?

You can, of course, sell fewer, more expensive items to get the same revenue, but I prefer new, small, cheap items which have high demand and sell many times each week, with a high profit per sale.

Example:

- An average product sells for $50.
- Each product sells 30 times per month.
- Revenue per product per month: $50 x 30 = $1,500.
- Revenue per product per annum: $1,500 x 12 = $18,000.
- Total revenue for 56 products is **$1,008,000** ($18,000 pa each product x 56 products = **$1,008,000.**)

Everybody starts their eBay business with zero products, and many of my students also started with zero money. (More on how to do this shortly).

To build a million dollar eBay business, simply keep adding more products (leaves) to your eBay tree, at your own speed, while using the profits to pay for them.

When building your business, always build it at a speed at which you feel comfortable. Just keep increasing the profits by adding more high-profit products to your business.

Now let me show you how you can start without spending a cent.

CHAPTER THREE

Which Products to Sell?

"Decide that you want it more than you are afraid of it."

~ BILL COSBY ~

eBay gives us the option to sell second-hand, used items as well as brand-new items. In the beginning, eBay was all about selling used items through its auction system, but the world is a different place now. Today, eBay buyers want more brand-new items than used items, and many will not wait for an auction to finish. They want to "Buy It Now," also know as BIN, on eBay.

Choosing between new or used products all comes down to how much experience you have with eBay, as well as how much working capital you have. Throughout this book, I will always assume the reader has zero experience and zero capital. If you have experience and/or working capital, then that is a bonus for you! If you don't have either, I will show you how to quickly gain both.

My preference for products these days are new, cheap, high-profit products. However, if you have no working capital, I will show you how to build some by using second-hand products, so that you can move on to new products when you accumulate enough capital.

The advantage of new products is you can buy *more than one* of the same *identical* item, but you only have to take one photo and create one ad. You can then sell the same identical items over and over again. With used items, you have to photograph each item individually, and then create one ad for that one item.

When most people start selling items on eBay, they generally begin by selling used items which are lying around the house, attic, garage, backyard, etc. My wife calls this 'Feng Shui clutter-clearing'. Never think something will not sell! The first item ever to sell on Auctionweb (which was later renamed to eBay) was listed for auction by founder Pierre Omidyar, and was a laser pointer which was clearly listed as "BROKEN". Regardless, it sold for $14!

There are thousands, if not millions, of people on eBay who are successfully selling items that seem like worthless - old things, like worn-out sandals, scratched CD's, broken toys, marked clothing, marked furniture, etc. These items sell all day, every day, on eBay. If it is lying around, turn it into profit on eBay, not only to gain some cash, but to gain valuable eBay experience as well.

Here are some items you may have lying around:

- Old televisions and remotes.
- Television cabinets.
- Chairs.
- Couches.
- Hi-fi equipment, e.g., VCR & DVD players, record players, etc. (Yep, people still buy these).
- Old game machines, like Nintendo, Xbox, etc.
- All video games, game machines and controllers can be sold separately or in bulk.

- Coffee tables.
- Video cameras, still cameras, camera lenses, etc.
- Headphones.
- Old mobile phones and PDA's.
- Unused computers, including desktops and notebooks.
- Computer monitors.
- Computer parts, including old hard drives, boards, modems, routers, etc.
- Sunglasses and prescription glasses.
- Watches.
- Lamps and lights.
- Bedside tables.
- Beds, including mattresses and bases.
- Clothes, including jackets, dress shoes, shirts, dress pants, jeans, swimsuits. (Brand names make the most money).
- Jewelry and accessories.
- Baby-ware, including strollers, bassinets, cots, diaper bags, baby toys, baby clothes, changing tables, feeding gear, etc.
- Children's toys.
- Hobbies (stamp collections, train sets, model airplane kits, woodworking, etc.).
- Children's clothing, including outgrown school uniforms, jeans, jumpers, jackets, shoes, and dresses. Again, brand names make the most money.
- Musical instruments, like guitars, keyboards, drum kits, amplifiers, etc.
- Comic books.
- Records.
- CD's.
- DVD's.
- Arts and crafts (beads, ceramics, jewelry-making, etc.).
- Wedding gear.
- Camping equipment.
- Books.
- Car parts, including car audio, owner's manuals, etc.

- Boat parts.
- Bicycles and bike parts.
- Skateboards and skateboard parts.
- Tools (both power tools and manual tools, like socket sets).
- Sporting equipment such as tennis rackets, golf clubs, baseball bats and gloves, motorbike gear, horse-riding gear, water sports equipment, snow skis, ice skates, rollerblades, etc.
- Collectables like number plates, old Coke bottles, etc.
- Stamp collections.
- Kitchenware such as: appliances, pots and pans, crockery, silverware, etc.
- Refrigerators.
- Washing machines.
- Clothes dryers.

No matter how much working capital you have, I HIGHLY RECOMMEND to anybody who is new to eBay: start off selling a few used items to gain experience. The lessons you will quickly learn are invaluable.

This is how we started, and it is how I always try to get my students to start. It is a fantastic introduction to eBay and a great way to turn unused items into cash while clearing some space in the house/garage/attic. This cash can be used later to buy some new, cheap, high-profit items.

The next way to get products for free is during "council clean ups" (a phrase which changes, depending on the country, i.e., in the U.S., this is referred to as "universal curbside bulky item collection"). On certain dates of the year, households are allowed to put large, unwanted items outside of their homes, and the local council removes it during roadside pickup. It is staggering what people throw out. One of my students regularly makes over $1,000 in one weekend from collecting these items.

Just a few examples of the thousands of things people throw out that can be sold on eBay:

- Hi-fi equipment, including speakers, which can be sold separately.
- Bicycles, particular vintage bikes and children's bikes.
- Surfboards.
- Snowboards.
- Coffee machines.
- Sewing machines.
- Exercise equipment, like weights, cross trainers, ab trainers, etc.
- Skateboards and skateboard parts.
- Old records
- Baby gear.

Council clean-ups normally move from one suburb to the next, adjoining suburb the following week. Once you find a cleanup, it is easy to find the next one on the following weekend. You can also contact local councils to find out the location of the next one.

Another source of free products is to offer to sell, on commission, used items for family and friends. Many people can't be bothered to list items on eBay, or they simply don't understand the process. They also vastly underestimate the value of the items they have lying around the house, collecting dust. Many of my students have done this in their early days, and they have received many referrals from their customers, which allow them to sell more items.

eBay Trading Assistant

Once you have gained some experience, you can also sign up to be an eBay Trading Assistant.

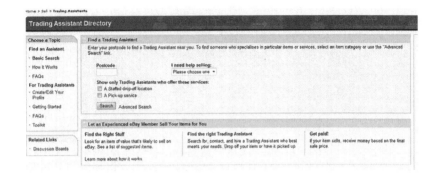

Once you are an eBay Trading Assistant, you can use your eBay skills to sell other people's items for a fee. The fee is negotiated between you and the owner of the items. Most of my coaching students charge between 5% for an expensive item like a vehicle, to 50% for cheaper items. It is purely up to you to choose your fee.

The secret to being successful at selling other people's items is to complete every single task for them. If they are too lazy to sell the items themselves, then they will almost certainly be too lazy to drop them off to you. If you do everything yourself, you can control the process, they will love you for it, and most importantly, they will give you more business. Most importantly, they will tell their friends about you.

People get very excited when you take something off their hands that is either not being used or that they paid virtually nothing for, especially when you return with cash!

Because you are providing a great service, you will build up your clientele, and before long, you will have a full-time, money-making business from home. Always keep in the back of your mind, however, that this is only a stepping stone for increasing knowledge, and for building up your bank balance, as the big money is in selling new, high-profit items.

To get onto eBay's Trading Assistant program, click on "Site Map," which is located on the bottom of any eBay page, and then click on "Trading Assistant," which is in the middle column:

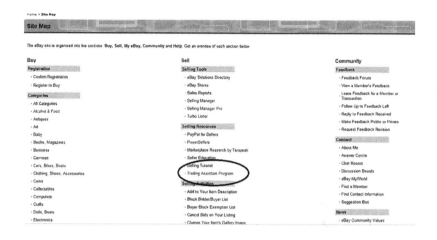

eBay Wholesale Lots

Another way of finding products is by scanning through the items on eBay's "Wholesale Lots." (See Image below).

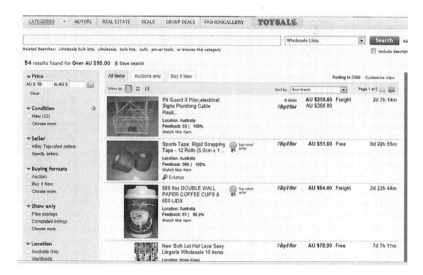

With wholesale lots, sellers can sell items in bulk. You can purchase these bulk deals and then sell the items individually.

Of course, always do your research first as to how much these items sell for individually, using the strategies in this book.

Personally, I am not a great fan of using eBay Lots, as once they are all sold, you normally cannot buy more, so all the effort you put in (of taking photos, writing ad copy, etc.) is now worthless.

To get to eBay Wholesale Lots, go to the eBay home page and click on "Categories."

Next, click on "Everything Else."

Finally, scroll down to "Wholesale Lots."

Music	Military Records	Other
Sex Accessories	Other	
Sex Toys		**Religious Products & Supplies**
Video Games	**Information Products**	Art
Other	How-To Guides	Bibles Covers & Accessories
	Wholesale Lists	Clothing
Advertising Opportunities	Other	Communion Accessories
		Crosses
eBay User Tools	**Memberships**	Educational Materials
		Jewelry
Education & Learning	Metaphysical	Judaica
Preschool-Kindergarten	Astrology	Rosaries
Elementary School	Crystal Healing	Other
Middle School	Feng Shui	
High School	Goth	**Reward Pts, Incentive Progs**
Adult & Career Education	Psychic, Paranormal	Proof of Purchase, UPCs
School Supplies, Equipment	Reiki	Reward Points
Teaching Supplies, Resources	Runes	Other
Wholesale Lots	Tarot	
Other	Wicca	**Weird Stuff**
	Other	Slightly Unusual
Funeral & Cemetery		Really Weird
Caskets		Totally Bizarre
Cemetery Plots		
Cremation Urns		**Other**
Mortuary Supplies		
Other		**Test Auctions**
		Attributes

Starting with Zero Money

To prove the theory of starting with zero money, we started by driving around clean-up campaigns (a.k.a. "council cleanups") and would then go home and list the items on eBay. I am sure some people will find it beneath them to start this way. Even so, I urge people to give it a go. Niq and I have very fond memories: we had a ball and learned a lot, too.

Garage Sales

When you are starting out, after you have raised some capital from the above methods, another good source for cheap products are

Saturday morning garage sales. (In some countries, these are called "car boot" sales). While collecting data for this book, we went to three of these on one Saturday morning, and here are the results:

Item	Cost Price	Sold on eBay	Profit
Sewing Machine	30	141	111
Video Camera	150	260	110
Wooden Puppet	2	27	25
Saxophone	10	280	270
Small Hi-fi	40	118	78
Sewing Machine	20	127	107
35 mm Camera	25	31	6
Total	$277	$983	$706

So, after three garage sales we made $706, which I reckon is a pretty good profit!

Other places to find used products are:

- Moving sales: Check local newspapers to find these.
- Church rummage sales: Check local newspapers to find these.
- Local charity fundraiser sales: Check local newspapers to find these.
- Auction sales - Check newspapers to find these.
- Flea markets.

New Products

The real big money is in low-cost, high-profit, new products, because you can take one picture and sell them over and over again. Some of our new products were photographed back in 2005, and they continue selling, over and over again. (With used items, you take the photo and write the ad; then sell it once). Also, most new items have an endless supply. On average, a new item sells for $46 dollars, but only costs $9.

We just keep adding more new products every month.

Recently, I attended an Internet summit in Maui, Hawaii, and was surprised by how many of the faces had changed. Sure, there are a few who attend every year, but most people don't, as their Internet business profits go up and down, with an emphasis on down. This had me wondering what the majority is doing differently from the minority, whose businesses were growing. The answer is extremely simple: The one-hit wonders have all their eggs in one basket, meaning if the market or competition changes, their businesses take a hit. Having all your eggs in one basket is not a great idea for any business person: the stress of always worrying about tomorrow can really take a toll on your health.

It's more fun, more relaxing, and more profitable to build a business with many different products (e.g., the money tree) as discussed in Chapter One.

What I love about new, high-profit products is that there is a never-ending supply of them. The great thing about eBay is that you can work out, pretty accurately, how much you will make BEFORE you sell anything. I will show you how, shortly. First, let's get clear on some basics.

When selling on eBay, everybody wants a bargain. For this reason, it is important to buy an item at the lowest price possible.

YOU MAKE YOUR MONEY WHEN YOU BUY AN ITEM -NOT WHEN YOU SELL IT.

"Profit" is the sale price minus the cost price (i.e., an item which sells for $50 and costs $20 creates a profit of $30). Another very important factor is "stock turn" (i.e., how many times an identical item sells per month). If a particular item sells 20 times in a month, the "stock turn" is 20. This means that you can make a $30 profit times a stock turn of 20 which equals $600 for the one product (e.g., $30 x 20 = $600).

The cost price is easy to find out: just ask the supplier. To find out the sale price for an item *before* you sell it, use the "Completed Listings" button in the eBay search results to reference the amount that the *same* item has previously sold for. For instance, you can see exactly how much items *have actually sold for* in the past on eBay by clicking on the "Completed Listings" button within eBay.

In my opinion, this is **THE MOST POWERFUL BUTTON** in eBay:

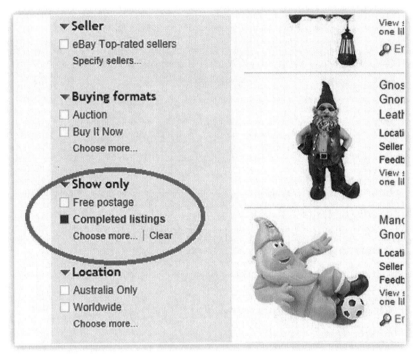

To explore, visit the eBay site in your country.

At the time of writing, eBay was located in 22 countries:

ASIA
Australia:	www.eBay.com.au
Hong Kong:	www.eBay.com.hk
India:	www.eBay.com.in
Malaysia:	www.eBay.com.my
New Zealand:	www.eBay.co.nz
Philippines:	www.eBay.ph
Singapore:	www.eBay.sg
South Korea:	www.eBay.co.kr

EUROPE
Austria:	www.eBay.at
Belgium:	www.eBay.be
France:	www.eBay.fr
Germany:	www.eBay.de
Ireland:	www.eBay.ie
Italy:	www.eBay.it
Netherlands:	www.eBay.nl
Poland:	www.eBay.pl
Spain:	www.eBay.es
Sweden:	www.eBay.se
Switzerland:	www.eBay.ch
United Kingdom:	www.eBay.co.uk

NORTH AMERICA
Canada:	www.eBay.ca
America:	www.eBay.com

To search for something on eBay, type in one of the URL's above (i.e., for the United States, type www.eBay.com into your browser; for eBay Italy, type www.eBay.it into your browser). Once you are on your local eBay website, find the search box within eBay as per the picture below:

In this example, I searched for "Garden Gnome":

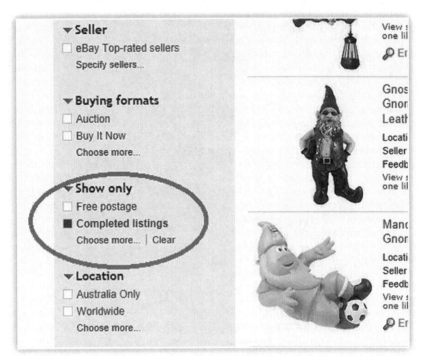

When eBay shows you the search results from your search, scroll down the left-hand side until you find the "Completed Listings" button. Check the button, and wait for eBay to update the results.

When results from a search are displayed, you can see that the prices in green were sold and the ones in red were not sold:

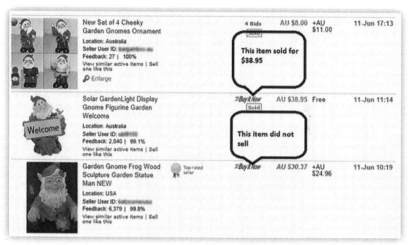

You can also search for completed listings using the "Advanced Search" option, as per the screenshot below:

To do this:

1. Click the "Advanced Search" button.
2. Type in the keywords for your search.
3. Click the "Completed Listings" button.
4. Click "Search."

There is a big difference between how much an item is *currently* selling for on eBay, and how much the identical item has *previously* sold for. Likewise, with eBay auctions, there is a big difference between how high-priced an auction item is now, and how high similar auction items *actually* sold for in the past. This is where the "Completed Listings" button comes in: Like most businesses, past history is the best prediction for the future.

What to Sell?

Every business on the planet sells either products or services. eBay, of course, is a product-based business, and with all product-based businesses, we need to be able to purchase an item for substantially less than it sells for in order to make the most profit.

Again, "profit" is the difference between how much an item costs and how much it sells for. Our calculation of an "arbitrage opportunity" is defined as profit times the number of times a product sells in one month (i.e., "Garden Gnome XYZ" sells on average for $50 and costs $20, creating a $30 profit; and sells 20 times per month, creating a monthly profit of $600. Therefore, the arbitrage opportunity for "Garden Gnome XYZ" is $600, meaning that there is an overall profit of $600 per month).

This is how we look at all new items:

- If we are researching new products to sell, we want to know the arbitrage opportunity: how much profit the product is generating per month.
- If the arbitrage opportunity is high (e.g., $600 per month), then we will consider ordering that product.

Going back to the tree, I think of each leaf on the tree as a separate arbitrage.

There are several ways to find arbitrages, from free strategies wherein you find the arbitrages yourself, to full-service strategies wherein you purchase arbitrages.

Let's start with the free strategies.

First of all, you need to choose a "niche." According to Wikipedia, a "niche market is the subset of the market on which a specific product is focusing." There are literally thousands of niches to choose from.

Some examples of "niches" are:

- Party accessories.
- Golf accessories.
- Sewing accessories.
- Bicycle accessories.
- Motorcycle accessories.
- Kitchen accessories.
- Clothing accessories.
- Boat accessories.
- Trailer accessories.
- Tools and hardware accessories.
- Bathroom accessories.
- Pet accessories.
- Baby accessories.

A fun place to start is to make a list of the niches you are passionate about (i.e., your hobbies and interests).

Ask yourself these questions and make notes:

- What is my favorite hobby?
- What do I find interesting?
- What other hobbies/interests have I had over the years?
- Which magazines have I purchased over the years?
- Which genre of books do I read/have read?
- What do I like to do on the weekends?
- Which courses have I attended?
- Which seminars have I attended?
- What do I do for work now, and in the past?

Another place to find niches is through popular press. Almost every magazine is built around a niche market (i.e., pregnancy = baby accessories, maternity clothes, etc.).

Still another place to find your niche is directly on eBay. Go to http://pulse.eBay.com and then scroll to the bottom where it says "Browse Categories."

When you click on "Browse Categories," you will see a page similar to the one below:

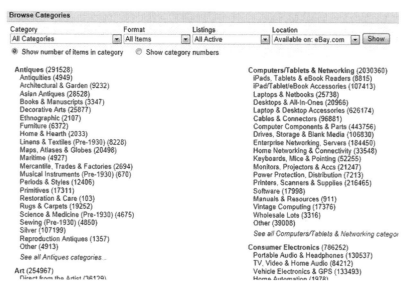

```
Browse Categories
Category              Format            Listings          Location
All Categories    ▼  All Items     ▼   All Active    ▼   Available on: eBay.com  ▼  Show
  ◉ Show number of items in category   ○ Show category numbers
```

Antiques (291528)   Computers/Tablets & Networking (2030360)
  Antiquities (4949)   iPads, Tablets & eBook Readers (8815)
  Architectural & Garden (9232)   iPad/Tablet/eBook Accessories (107413)
  Asian Antiques (28528)   Laptops & Netbooks (25738)
  Books & Manuscripts (3347)   Desktops & All-In-Ones (20966)
  Decorative Arts (25877)   Laptop & Desktop Accessories (626174)
  Ethnographic (2107)   Cables & Connectors (96881)
  Furniture (6372)   Computer Components & Parts (443756)
  Home & Hearth (2033)   Drives, Storage & Blank Media (106830)
  Linens & Textiles (Pre-1930) (8228)   Enterprise Networking, Servers (184450)
  Maps, Atlases & Globes (20498)   Home Networking & Connectivity (33548)
  Maritime (4927)   Keyboards, Mice & Pointing (52255)
  Mercantile, Trades & Factories (2694)   Monitors, Projectors & Accs (21247)
  Musical Instruments (Pre-1930) (670)   Power Protection, Distribution (7213)
  Periods & Styles (12406)   Printers, Scanners & Supplies (216465)
  Primitives (17311)   Software (17998)
  Restoration & Care (103)   Manuals & Resources (911)
  Rugs & Carpets (19252)   Vintage Computing (17376)
  Science & Medicine (Pre-1930) (4675)   Wholesale Lots (3316)
  Sewing (Pre-1930) (4850)   Other (39008)
  Silver (107199)   *See all Computers/Tablets & Networking categor*
  Reproduction Antiques (1357)
  Other (4913)   Consumer Electronics (786252)
  See all Antiques categories...   Portable Audio & Headphones (130537)
                                                       TV, Video & Home Audio (84212)
Art (254967)   Vehicle Electronics & GPS (133493)
  Direct from the Artist (36129)   Home Automation (1978)

This is only a snippet of all of the categories, and each category has sub-categories. Each sub-category is another niche.

Let's say you choose the "Bathroom Accessories" niche. The next step is to find arbitrages for bathroom accessories. To do this, use eBay pulse as above (http://pulse.eBay.com), then click on "Bath," which is a sub-category under "Home & Garden":

See all Home Entertainment categon

Home & Garden (45854)
Bathroom (13024)
Bedding (17304)
Building Materials, DIY (46346)
Cleaning, Housekeeping (4508)
Curtains, Blinds (6290)
Environmental Solutions (341)
Furniture (29599)

After clicking on "Bath," you will see all of the items in the "Bath" sub-category.

Next, click on the "Completed listings" button which is located half way down the left side:

Now, sort by "highest first" using the "Sort by" button:

(The prices which are green have sold; the ones in red did not sell).

As all the items are now sorted by price, scroll down to where the most expensive item is, say, $35.

Following this example, make a list of about 10 to 20 items which sold for more than $20 but less than $35. Set the maximum at $150 (because, on average, we find that items over $150 sell more slowly, and we want fast-selling, high-profit items).

When searching for products, I highly recommend using the following criteria:

- All products must be family-friendly (i.e., no adult products).
- No brand names, as these can be fakes! eBay will not tolerate fakes, and can suspend and even shut you down for repeat offenses.
- Choose items which sell for more than $20 and less than $150. We do make some exceptions to this rule based on how profitable an item is and how many times it sells in a month (stock turn).
- Must sell, on average, more than 10 times per month.
- Must generate greater than 100% profit per sale.
- Non-seasonal, i.e., do not sell Christmas lights.
- No time-limited products such as iPhone cases, which become obsolete when the next model iPhone arrives.

When you begin, only look for small items that can be mailed easily. Avoid heavy and/or bulky items, such as heaters, childrens' backyard swing sets, barbeques, etc.

Don't try for the home run! Just find products that match your criteria. You are much better off having many small products which turn a good profit than one big, expensive product.

Another warning: Remember the phrase "Paralysis by analysis." That is, don't get too bogged down in researching products. They either meet the criteria or they don't. Quickly make the decision and move on. Do not let your emotions get in the way. It is irrelevant whether you or I like the color, model, etc. The product either meets the criteria or it doesn't. Let the data make the decisions.

When you find an item that works with the criteria above, the next step is to find out how many times it has sold in the last 30 days.

Just now, I ran a quick search. The first item I found is a "Triple Soap Shampoo Lotion Dispenser Wall Mounted New" (below):

Triple Soap Shampoo Lotion Dispenser Wall Mounted NEW
See original listing

Item condition: **Brand New**
Ended

Sold For: **AU $35.00** [30 sold]
Postage: **FREE**

From the screenshot above, you can see it has sold 30 times since it was *listed*, but it may have been listed six months ago, so further research is necessary.

Click on the "[30 sold]" (the number will change with every different item) and you will see how many times this item sold in the last 30 days. Make a note of it.

Next, search for identical items and see how many of those sold as well. We just need a minimum of ten sales per month to prove that the item is in demand.

To find other identical items, go to eBay and in the eBay search box, type the keywords which are in the title (e.g., "triple soap dispenser").

Be careful not to use too many keywords for your search, as the more keywords you use, the less search results you get. Alternatively, do not use too few keywords, as you will retrieve too many results. Let me show you.

This is an example of the amount of results I got from three similar searches:

Keyword(s)	Results
soap	76,340
soap dispenser	4,580
soap shampoo dispenser	124
triple soap shampoo dispenser	6

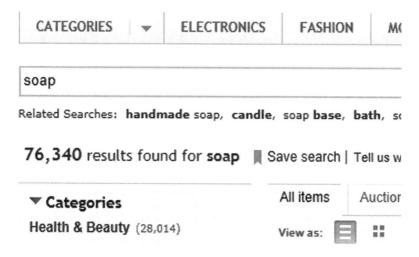

Once you have chosen some products which meet the criteria in the filters, it is time to source them from suppliers.

Let's use the above example of the "Triple Soap Shampoo Dispenser" which, from my research above, sells (on average) for $35, and has sold 17 times in the last 30 days.

When sourcing products, to make the most profit, you need to buy at the lowest possible price.

Remember:

YOU MAKE YOUR MONEY WHEN YOU BUY AN ITEM -NOT WHEN YOU SELL IT.

For this reason, I do not like drop shipping as the drop shipper makes most of the profit.

Over 90% of the new items sold on eBay come from China, and these days it is easy to buy direct from China. Some people are afraid to buy from China as they would be "importers," and they believe you need a mountain of licenses and money to do this.

Nothing could be further from the truth! They also believe there is a strong chance of losing their money. Again, this is not the case as long as you follow some simple steps, which I will show you.

Have you ever sent $20 to Grandma, or a friend in another country, and asked them to mail you an XYZ? If you have, and it arrived in your mailbox, then you are already an importer! Congratulations.

> *"Many of our fears are tissue-paper-thin, and a single courageous step would carry us clear through them."*

~BRENDAN FRANCIS ~

These days, almost all of the products that Niq and I purchase come from China, and we import them all ourselves. You can, too.

Because most of the suppliers in China use USD (U.S. Dollars), to keep things simple, I will also use USD. To convert USD to another currency, just go to XE's free online currency conversion at www.xe.com. To find products in China, you can use either www.globalsources.com or www.alibaba.com. We prefer Alibaba, however it is just a personal preference.

In the Alibaba search box, type in some keywords to find your item, e.g., "shampoo dispensers":

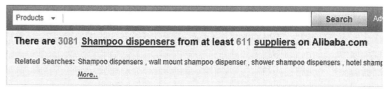

Home > Products > Construction & Real Estate > Bathroom > Bathroom Accessories > Liquid Soap Dispensers (22317)

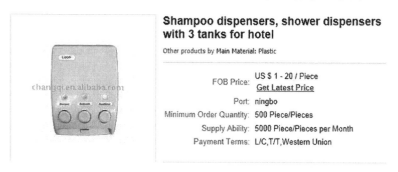

As you can see above, I found the identical dispenser. Now click on the "Get Latest Price" link to request a price from the supplier.

The next consideration is the MOQ (minimum order quantity). Do not be put off if the MOQ is very high (e.g. 500). The Chinese LOVE to negotiate, and will very often send samples (smaller amounts like six or ten units). Sometimes they will even give you free samples. Just email them and negotiate for what you want. Remember: Price and MOQ are *always* negotiable. Negotiate, negotiate, negotiate! Always negotiate through email, as it is far easier and much less stressful than over the phone.

Often, a lower MOQ can be offset by a slightly higher price. Alternatively, a higher MOQ can be offset by a lower price. Take your time! So what if it takes five emails and one week to negotiate a great price and a lower MOQ? After two emails I negotiated an MOQ down from 500 to 20 for a cost price of $5 each.

Make sure you email the supplier to confirm prices and MOQ. Chinese suppliers are always willing to negotiate for better deals, and are especially flexible with the MOQ. Moreover, as mentioned above, many manufacturers will supply samples at very small quantities.

If ever a supplier does not respond to your emails, try calling them on the phone. If you are not happy with the response times from a supplier, move on to a different product. Do not get emotionally attached to one product or one supplier! There are literally thousands, if not millions, of new, hot, highly profitable items, so don't waste time on an unhelpful supplier. On the whole, most suppliers are pleasant to deal with, and eager to preserve your business.

For your first order, order samples only. This will bypass the MOQ. Again, the Chinese love to negotiate, and these days, considering various language barriers, negotiating by email is much easier than over the phone.

If you are building the business to make money, do not put massive limits on your product ranges by *only* choosing a product for emotional reasons or because you "like it." Let the facts and figures dictate which products your business sells (as long as the product is ethical).

When importing items from China, be VERY careful about importing items with brand names, as there is a very high chance they will be imposters (i.e., "Rolex" watches for $20, or "Gucci" handbags for $10. Even much simpler products, like 50-cent batteries, can have a well-known name brand printed on them but are actually fakes). *We very rarely import items with brand names* due to the high risk that they are scams. We make exceptions only after thoroughly vetting the supplier to ensure that the items are 100% original. It really is a lot easier to forego importing items with brand names altogether, as there are so many unique products to choose from instead. You do not want to build your business on quicksand!

Always make sure that the supplier is credible. Our minimum criteria is that a supplier is classified as "Gold" for at least two years. (Alibaba makes this process really easy).

As per the pic below, this supplier has been verified by Alibaba and has been a gold member for 6 years:

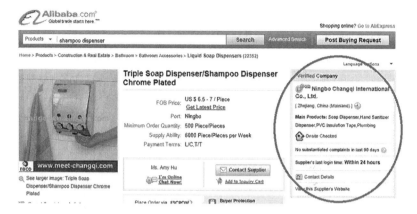

Here is an excerpt from Alibaba, defining the criteria for "Gold" status:

Gold Supplier is a premium membership for suppliers on Alibaba.com. It provides an extensive number of promotional opportunities to maximize their exposure and return-on-investment. To qualify for a Gold Supplier membership, a supplier must complete an authentication and verification process by a reputable third-party security service provider appointed by Alibaba.com. Once approved, Gold Supplier members are authorized to display the icon to demonstrate their authenticity.

For more information, go to:
http://static.alibaba.com/hermes/goldsuppliers.html

Shipping from China

I prefer to think of this as just 'post', as it really is just normal post. Most suppliers will ship using the courier of your choice; we prefer EMS air freight (air mail). Just like regular mail, your imports will arrive at your front door via your local postal system. Airfreight is the most expensive (as compared with shipping items by sea) but it is also the fastest option, and for small orders, the most economical.

Many multi-million dollar eBay businesses *only* use EMS, *however*, they only import small items. Air freight will *not work* for heavy or bulky items (e.g. a barbeque) as the cost of shipping a barbeque will normally be greater than the profit. Airfreight only works with small, lightweight items.

From China to most countries, the normal delivery time is approximately 10 days, but check with the supplier to your country. In most countries, most small orders will normally slide under the radar, and will arrive at your front door without the use of a freight forwarder. Regardless, always check with a freight forwarder (i.e., a third-party agent for the cargo industry) for your country's legal and tax requirements.

Most suppliers will send goods "FOB" (Freight on Board). That is, they will pay the postal charges on your behalf. This widely-used term comes from the sea freight industry, meaning if the supplier sends something FOB, they will pay the shipping costs *to* your country (but not any of the costs accrued *in* your country). Once the goods arrive, however, the unloading costs are not included. When requesting a quote from a supplier, always ask for the FOB price, as this will include your shipping costs. (FOB also applies to air freight, meaning that the supplier also pays the air freight shipping charges for you, but not any of the charges incurred once the items arrive).

Small airfreight orders normally arrive at your front door with no extra charges; however larger airfreight shipments (if stopped by customs) will attract charges. Again, Google a local freight forwarder in your country, and ask them what charges, if any, you will need to pay.

Until you have grown your business and have the necessary cash flow and experience to import larger quantities by sea, always import smaller items, as it is expensive to ship bulky and or heavy items by air.

When you have grown large enough, you will begin using sea freight for large orders. Sea freight delivery takes approximately one to four weeks, depending on which country you are located in.

There are two ways to get items sent by sea: by FCL (Full Container Load) or LCL (Less than Container Load).

- FCL (Full Container Load) is the most economical, as the container is packed in China with only your items, and then delivered - unopened - to your front door.
- LCL (Less than Container Load) means that your goods are *part* of a larger shipment, i.e., you share a container with others.

To get prices for sea freight, request an FOB price from the supplier; then ask the freight forwarder for local costs and taxes.

To give you a rough idea, from China to Australia, for a 20-foot container, the cost is approximately $1,800 USD for sea freight plus $1,000 for local charges (i.e., the freight forwarder, dock fees, truck transport fees, etc.). Like air freight, the cost of shipping is then divided among all of the products in the shipment: If there are 3,000 items in the container and the container costs $3,000, the price will be $1 in freight for each product.

Of course, this is supposing that all items were the same size.

The cost to purchase enough goods to fill a container varies, beginning at around $2,000. It just depends on the price of the item, the time of shipment, and how many items you can fit in the container. For instance, if you imported large canoes which cost, say, $100 each, you may be able to fit 20 canoes into a 20-foot container, which would cost $2,000. On the other hand, if you imported much smaller items, say, the size of watches, at around $5 each, you would be able to fit approximately 10,000 watches into a 20-foot container, costing $50,000 for the stock. We call this "container density."

You *can* have bulkier or heavier items shipped by air, however, the cost of air mail will eat the profit.

There is one exception to this rule:

For samples, it does not matter if the airfreight eats into the profit as the main shipment can be sent by sea.

Prohibited Items on eBay

At the end of this section, you will find a list of items that are banned from eBay, but the fastest way to discover if an item is prohibited is to see if any of the big sellers are selling - or rather, *not* selling - the same item on eBay already.

For example, one product which came up for us a while back was an exercise machine called the "Ab Circle Pro." Our initial data showed that these were selling, on average, for $215 each, and that we could purchase what seemed to be the same item for less than $30. This all looked okay, but when we searched eBay in the USA, UK, Canada, and Australia for "Ab Circle Pro," we only found small sellers with low feedback ratings (less than 300). This immediately sent off alarm bells. Why weren't the big sellers offering this product? Were we the only people to make this huge arbitrage discovery? Not likely!

When a scenario like this happens, the next step is to check for trademarks at http://www.trademarkia.com

Using the search box in Trademarkia, we searched for Ab Circle Pro, and sure enough, the words "Ab Circle Pro" are trademarked:

If we had ordered these and then listed them on eBay, I guarantee the owners of the Ab Circle Pro trademark would have

immediately contacted eBay to report us for selling a counterfeit product, and eBay would have had no choice but to shut down our listings for these items, and to issue us an official warning.

Small eBay sellers are getting around this dilemma by incorporating the phrase "unused gift" in their advertisements, effectively building businesses on quicksand - if you try this sort of strategy, eBay will catch you and shut you down.

Prohibited Items

- Guns, firearms, and military weapons.
- Human parts and remains.
- Police, government, and various law enforcement agency ID's, including replications.
- Vehicle license plates less than five years old. (License plates older than five years are regarded as collectable, and are thus allowed).
- Lock-picking tools and devices.
- Drugs and drug paraphernalia.
- Prescription drugs.
- Stocks, bonds or negotiable securities.
- Bulk email lists.
- Pets and wildlife.
- Pornography.
- Forged items, e.g., forged signatures on posters, etc.
- Items which infringe on copyright and/or trademarks.
- Illegal copies of movies or music.
- Worn underwear.
- Recalled items.
- Stolen items.

Bottom line: if you research new items and there are no large eBay sellers (1,000 + feedbacks) anywhere on the planet selling the same item, then let that be a HUGE alert for you.

Note: Occasionally, some items that are banned in one country can be listed on eBay in another.

Ordering Checklist

Our first step is to make sure that the supplier is legit. Then we check to ensure that the product meets our criteria:

1. No wood products unless you are prepared to go through the declarations to import wooden products. If you do wish to import wooden products, check with your local customs in regards to the procedure for declaring wooden items.
2. No brand names unless you are 110% sure it is not a Chinese knock-off. The Chinese are renowned for making fake brand name items. It is safer to avoid importing brand names altogether.
3. Make sure the supplier has their own website.
4. Make sure the supplier uses an email address from their own domain name and not a hotmail (etc.) email address.
5. Make sure the company has an advertised landline number on their website in addition to their mobile number.
6. Make sure that all companies have been in operation for at least two years using Alibaba's Gold Member program.
7. Before ordering, make sure you have received a quote with a "manufacturer's model number." Confirm that the model number is the exact same product.
8. To eliminate errors, always use the manufacturer's model number when ordering.

Arbitrage Tools

Tools reduce the time and effort to achieve results. A carpenter can manually hammer in nails one by one, or he can use a nail gun to speed up the process. If the carpenter is paid by the hour, then the hammer works just fine. If the carpenter is paid by the job, a nail gun is indispensable.

This principle applies to all different types of businesses, including eBay. Just as a carpenter should learn how to manually hammer a nail before mastering a nail gun, I believe that everybody should learn how to find arbitrages manually before using more advanced tools of technology. Even if you already have a million dollars in the bank, I highly recommend that you learn the manual process first, by implementing the above examples, before using any of the following tools below.

Terapeak

Terapeak is an eBay research tool to assist in finding the most popular items. It can also be used to help write ads, find the top sellers for different products, find average prices, and for a multitude of other tasks. The best way to learn about Terapeak is to watch their online training videos at: http://www.tera-peak.com

Waterhouse Research

Until 2011, we kept Waterhouse Research (WR) top secret, and only used the research data for our own eBay businesses and a few of my coaching clients. Today, it is the world's largest supplier of complete eBay arbitrages.

Waterhouse Research is a data center which tracks over 4 billion keywords every week to find which keywords end in a sale. The data is then fed through over 60,000 filters, and then matched to suppliers' products through a database of over 2 million products.

WR supplies eBay arbitrages which match the following criteria:

- Family-friendly products, (i.e., no adult products).
- No brand names.
- Gross profit must be greater than 100%.
- Average sale price must be greater than $30 and less than $150, barring special circumstances (e.g., very high profit).
- Low competition.
- Each arbitrage is supplied to one customer only, in order to limit competition.

For more information, go to: http://www.waterhouseresearch.com

CHAPTER FOUR

Photographing a Product

"When a man throws an empty cigarette package from an automobile, he is liable to a fine of $50. When a man throws a billboard across a view, he is richly rewarded."

~ GOVERNOR PAT BROWN (OGILVY ON ADVERTISING, 1985) ~

A good, clear studio quality photo is very important, and is a critical element in getting the most profit. The good news is that it is very easy to take "studio" quality pictures with almost any cheap digital camera.

You do not need the latest whiz-bang, ultra-high resolution, mega-expensive camera with a gazillion megapixel resolution and 100 trillion colors. After all, the Internet can only show 256 colors, and eBay reduces all the pictures you upload to a resolution of 800 x 600 pixels, which is less than half of 1 megapixel (800 x 600 = 480,000 pixels).

Today you would be hard-pressed to buy a new camera with less than 10 megapixels resolution! The cheapest camera from a reputable company like Canon (etc.) will be more than good enough. You *do* need to make sure the camera has a macro mode, manual exposure/shutter settings, the ability to turn the flash off, and a tripod mount. Most cheap cameras do have all of these features.

Note: It is illegal to copy anyone else's photos or any other company's photos, including eBay's, unless you have prior permission. If you copy any of your competitor's photos from eBay and then use them in your own listings, and you are reported, eBay will suspend all of your listings. If you are a repeat offender, eBay can terminate your account.

Likewise, if you catch anyone else using your photos, report them immediately to eBay, and eBay will shut down their listings.

Here's some good news. Usually, your competitors will use the exact same photos from the manufacturer of an item. By taking your own photo, yours will stand out from the crowd. Very often, the manufacturer's photos are not the type of photos which get the best prices. For instance, on average, photos which have clean, white, empty backgrounds sell more often, and achieve higher prices at auctions, than pictures with backgrounds.

This is so much the case that there are thousands of professional eBayers out there who search for items on auctions that have bad photos and/or bad ad copy. They do this, just so that they can buy them - cheap - and then relist them back on eBay with a better photo and better ad copy.

High quality pictures are critical, yet so very easy to create when you know how.

Be very careful if a manufacturer sends you photos to use in your listings, as these are, very often, taken by an in-house graphic artist who believes that the more razzamatazz in the photo, the better. Graphic artists love to make photographs "look" good; *however*, we need photographs which generate sales: There is a MASSIVE difference between the two. Fancy graphics in your photographs will only make them "look" better (to some people) but, as a general rule, they will reduce sales, often quite dramatically.

We have tested this theory over and over again - not just on eBay, but on our non-eBay websites (which sell exactly the same products as our eBay businesses). We have also split tested white backgrounds on websites against fancy backgrounds. The tests prove, over and over, that the best thing to have in a photo, and around your product, is a plain white background.

Buyers love to see the product by itself in photographs, with nothing in the background.

The best example of white background usage is the most popular - and the most split tested - website on the planet: Google. The most-used section of the Google website is the search box. Notice what is around the search box?

Yep, a whole lot of white.

The second largest website on the planet is Amazon. Notice their background, too.

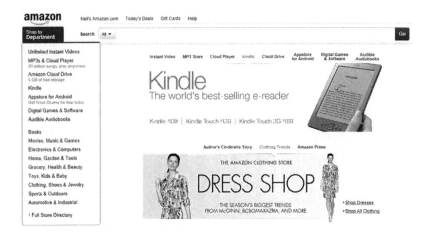

Lots more white

How to Take Clear, Crisp Pictures

To get those crisp photos, it is important to keep the camera steady by using either a tripod or a substitute for a tripod to rest the camera on. We keep several cut pieces of timber at different sizes, and also a small bag of rice, in our light tents (more on light tents further down). The rice bag is brilliant for resting a camera on, as it instantly molds to whatever it is resting on, as well as molding to the camera itself.

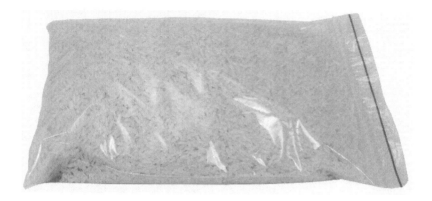

Above: Literally, a bag of rice. A cloth bag is even better than this Ziploc bag, as it is not as slippery. If you use a zip bag like this one, make sure you puncture the bag with at least 10 pinpricks so the air can escape when you rest the camera on it.

Above: Three different size pieces of timber for supporting the camera. (The cup shown is to illustrate the size of the pieces). The timber can be used vertically or stacked horizontally like kids' building blocks. It is amazing how many heights you can get with these blocks. You can, of course, cut whatever size you like. We much prefer this method in the light tent than a conventional tripod, as it is much faster. However, if the camera is used outside of the light tent, a tripod is normally the best option:

Conventional Camera Tripod

Years ago, I took a course on digital photography, only to discover that 90% of the lessons were not useful for our eBay businesses – a bit like taking a course on Microsoft Word so you can print a one-page letter. My guess is, most people understand less than 5% of what Microsoft Word can do, but most people are able to create what they need.

My task for this book is to try to keep things simple, and just focus on what is required to achieve results: in this case, to create studio quality pictures with the minimum amount of time and/or expense.

Out of all the zillions of functions digital cameras can do, we use only 3.

1. Macro: for taking photos of items when the item is less than 1 meter (3 feet) from the camera lens.
2. Exposure setting: This setting allows you to manually make the Image and background lighter and darker.
3. Flash control: Using the flash can make photos appear washed out and lacking in detail; it can also create glare, shadows and reflections. The best way for you to learn the difference between using lighting or the built-in flash is to take a picture with and without flash.

Not using the flash makes it even more critical to keep the camera still, as the lower light (i.e., no flash) requires the camera shutter to be open for longer. The longer the shutter is open, the more movement the <Insert Image gets, and the blurrier the picture becomes.

Never use zoom: always move the camera closer. Make sure the item completely fills the viewfinder by moving the camera closer.

For whatever digital camera you have, either dig out the manual or Google how to use the three settings above with YOUR camera.

Camera Manufacturer's

It seems everybody has their own opinion about which camera is best. Personally, I like Canon, however this is only because I am used to them, and the software for all the Canon cameras I have used is very similar.

Don't get too caught up in becoming a photo genius as it is not required – unless, of course, you love photography!

When sourcing new products, first ask suppliers to email you photos, but if they cannot supply the photo(s) or the photos are unusable (i.e., watermarked, or they do not have clean, white backgrounds), then you will need to take new photos yourself.

When taking photos for eBay, always take photos with a clean, white background (i.e., a white sheet or white wall).

Never have things in the background, i.e., childrens' toys, kitchen items, etc. We have done exhaustive testing on this, and a clean, white background almost always outsells anything else.

If you would like to convey through the photo how small or large an item is, put something next to the item to illustrate the fact (i.e., if you are trying to convey it is small, put a ruler or a coin next to the item. If you would like to show how large it is, have somebody hold it. If you take a LOT of photos of large items, buy yourself a mannequin from eBay. This way, you do not continually require the services of somebody else.

Make sure the area is well lit - natural sunlight is suitable. Later on, you can go all out and set up a light tent (pictured below), however, this is not critical.

There are three ways to get perfect "studio" quality photos with perfect white backgrounds:

1. Set up a light tent like the one below:

2. Remove the background with photo editing software. (I will show you how you can use free software to do this).

3. Use a white sheet or white cardboard as a background.

With a light tent, the nylon material diffuses the lighting from external lights so that the light is distributed evenly around the item, and the shadows are greatly softened and reduced.

A light tent literally looks like a tent. My kids thought it was for camping! When we got our first light tent, as soon as we unfolded it, in hopped the kids, and the dog!

Regarding lights: you can read a lot about different "color temperatures," but we have found we get very similar results using fluorescent lights with a color temp between 3500 and 5000, as long as all of the lights are the same. The "white balance" on digital cameras can be adjusted to match whatever shade of white light you use.

There are many light tents and accessories listed on eBay, and there are many different sizes for photographing small items (e.g., jewelry) and larger items (e.g., full-size chairs). Again, you can do amazing things with a white sheet if you do not wish to spend money on a light tent.

Some people even make a light "cube" from a cardboard box, using cheap home light bulbs, which they purchase from their local grocery stores. However, make sure they are fluorescent lights; not the old incandescent lights, which are yellow when compared with fluorescent lights. Below: a typical, screw-in fluorescent light bulb.

These days, we use three different methods to photograph items, all of which depend on the size of the product.

1. For small items, we use a square light box which we purchased from Ortery. This is quite an expensive item, at over $5,000, and you only need something like this when you are photographing many items in one day. We justified the cost of the purchase by the savings in labour. Again, you do not need this when you start out, and you only need it if you are listing a lot of small items, like jewelry. The reason this light box is so expensive is that it comes automated with its own computer-run software, which operates the camera internally. The camera is fixed inside the light box, and all of the operations (like zoom, etc.) are controlled from the computer. This is a great gadget, and saves a lot of time, as the photos rarely need any editing; however, it is definitely not essential for an eBay business. You can get a very similar result using a cardboard box lined with white paper and a couple of cheap light bulbs; and then editing the photo using MS Paint.

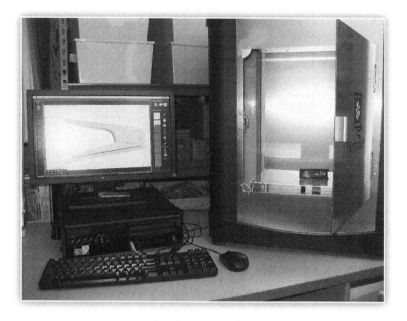

Our Ortery light box

2. For larger items, we use a 1.5 meter square light tent, like the one pictured above. We purchased this from eBay many years ago, and it works well.

3. For larger items, we use a large piece of material which we purchased from a local fabric store, and a couple of lights from eBay. A white sheet is a sufficient piece of white material. You can push a table against a wall, hang a white sheet (or white paper) from the top of the wall, and then curve it to the front edge of the table. This produces a seamless, white background.

Editing Photos

The photo on the following page was taken before editing. Notice that the background is gray despite the fact that the picture was actually taken using a white background. This background could have been made whiter by increasing the exposure on the camera; however, too much exposure will lower the detail of the item. You can experiment with the exposure settings on your camera to see this for yourself.

Before Digitally Removing the Background:

After Digitally Removing the Background:

To get the "studio" look with no background, you can use a photo editing program. Again, keep it simple: you do not need to become an editing genius; all you need to know is the exact buttons in the software to press to get the result you need.

To simplify the process, I have recorded some two minute, user-friendly videos which demonstrate all the steps that you need to know. These are free to watch, and I will include the links later in this chapter.

Photoshop is the industry standard for professional photo editing software. It has every function known to mankind, and probably a zillion more too - definitely overkill for what we need.
Photoshop Elements is the stripped-down version of Photoshop. Elements can do everything an eBay trader needs and more, however, you do not need to rush out and buy either version of Photoshop. You can simply use Microsoft Paint, which comes free with every Windows PC, or Microsoft's Picture Manager, which comes free with Microsoft Office.

Most digital cameras also come with photo editing software, however, Microsoft Paint and Picture Manager are normally easier to use.

If you are interested in Photoshop Elements, you can download a free, 30-day trial at www.adobe.com

Here are the links to everything you need to know about removing backgrounds from photos:
Photoshop:
http://www.waterhouseresearch.com/coaching/photoshop
Photoshop Elements:
http://www.waterhouseresearch.com/coaching/elements
Microsoft Paint:
http://www.waterhouseresearch.com/coaching/mspaint

Quantity of Photos

The amount of photos you take of an item depends on how complex the item is: The more "features" the product has, the more pictures you should take.

Your goal is to try to answer as many of the future customer's questions as you can through pictures. Remember the old saying: "A picture speaks a thousand words."

This is most definitely true with eBay. Not only will you receive less questions (as buyers can work out the answers by looking at the photos), but you will also sell more items and for higher amounts. We have proven this, over and over. More pictures produce higher prices, more sales, and fewer questions.

eBay now allows us to upload up to 12 pictures onto eBay for free. Take as many photos as you need to capture all the features and benefits of an item. Our rule is, if an item has a feature or a benefit: photograph it. If it has a button, a light, a plug, a dial, a signature, a specific marking, etc., photograph it. The more features and benefits you show through your pictures, the more sales you will get, as well as higher auction prices. With some products, like T-shirts, you can tell the whole story with one photo; however, other items, like a multifunction kitchen blender, will require the whole twelve.

Previously, eBay charged an additional fee for multiple photos. To get around paying extra fees for extra photos, most serious eBay sellers would host the pictures on an external server in order to save money. eBay picture hosting fees would add up, making external hosting much cheaper.

Today, eBay makes life much easier by letting us upload 12 pictures for free. Not only is it easier, it is now critical to host pictures on eBay, as ONLY pictures which are uploaded on eBay will appear on smartphones and iPads (when users have downloaded the eBay app).

Watermarks

Watermarks protect your images from being copied by placing a semi-transparent Image of your name over every picture. Software like Photoshop can watermark your photos, however, don't overdo the watermark. There is nothing more annoying than looking at a picture of something you want to buy, and seeing a great, big, fat watermark all over it.

We prefer to take the risk of putting a small, semi-transparent watermark in the bottom corner of our images, even though someone could copy the picture and edit the watermark out with Photoshop. We would rather do this than lose sales because of big, ugly watermarks slapped all over our pictures.

Taking Advantage of Tax Perks From Working at Home

Claiming Purchases

Your eBay business is a real business; therefore, you can claim any business-related purchases, such as photography equipment, as tax deductions, as well as claiming any tax paid on inventory purchases. Always keep every receipt for every purchase.

You can also claim:

- Phones and phone bills for landlines and mobile phones.
- Internet bills.
- eBay fees.
- Bank fees.
- Electricity bills.
- Rent for the parts of your house you are using.
- Computer hardware.
- Computer software.
- Books for business (like this one).

- Printer costs.
- Camera equipment.
- Staff to help you.
- Office supplies.
- Car expenses for business use (i.e., trips to the post office, office supply store, department stores to research products, etc.).
- Gas for transportation.
- Office furniture.
- Seminars (eBay/Internet related).
- Travel to seminars, including flights and accommodation. (You can also take a vacation while at the seminar location and let the business pay for the flights, and the accommodations, during seminar dates).
- Education courses, like an evening course to learn Photoshop.
- Interest on credit cards if they were used to purchase inventory.
- Office food and drink.

The tax benefits are significant, because everything you do not have to pay income tax for is extra money in your pocket. In layman's terms: Say you earn a wage of $50,000 a year, and then pay $10,000 in income tax. This leaves you – an individual - with only $40,000. If you buy a personal computer (for say, $1,000), this, too, comes out of the $40,000.

In contrast, businesses only pay taxes on the leftover profit AFTER paying for all the expenses.

To illustrate, let's say your eBay business also makes $50,000, and it also buys a computer for $1,000. The $1,000 comes out from the $50,000 profit BEFORE taxes, leaving $49,000 in profit. The business then only pays tax on the leftover profit (i.e., the $49,000). This is why you should pay as many expenses as possible through the business.

Many businesses even claim more expenses than they make in profit for the first few years, meaning that they pay no tax at all.

Rent

In regards to claiming rent for your at-home business: in some countries, if you claim rent for the rooms of your house in which you conduct business, you may have to pay some capital gains tax, but ONLY for the period you claim. There is, however, another side to this argument.

If the price of real estate is not growing in your country (as it is not in most countries at the time of writing), then there is no capital gain to pay tax on anyway - so you may as well claim that part of the house.

For example: Let's say you have a mortgage of $2,500 per month and you can prove, through photographs, that you are using 50% of your house (and garage) for your eBay business. This means that you can channel 50% of the $2,500 ($1,250) through the business.

By doing this, you will not have to pay taxes on the $1,250 (which is paid by the business) because it is an expense.

This means that you, yourself, do not have to pay the $1,250 per month ($15,000 per year), including the additional tax of 25% per month (or whatever tax rate you are on), which saves you an additional $3,750. (25% tax on $1,250 is $313.50 x 12 months = $3,750).

As a secondary bonus, your personal income has now dropped $15,000 for the year, which could now place you in a lower tax bracket.

So personally, you now only have to pay $1,250 for the mortgage out of your *after*-tax dollar amount, which is now at a lower tax rate, due to your income decreasing by $15,000. Consequently, your income tax rate will be much less, as you will not only claim the rent, but all of the other expenses too.

After accounting for lower tax rates, this is just one scenario in which claiming rent can save you from paying nearly $4,000 in taxes for the year!

Talk to your accountant about this, but do not be immediately put off by "capital gains tax" when, in most places, there is either zero, or at most an insignificant amount, due to negative capital growth.

Note: Tax rules are different in every country. Always ask your accountant for what you can and cannot claim in your country.

By running a home business and claiming all of the many allowable deductions, you end up paying much less in taxes, so you end up making more money as you do not have to write that extra check to the government.

Most of my students don't get the concept of claiming expenses through their home business, consequently paying less in taxes, and thus increasing their income, until it is really explained to them.

Most people I speak to think that channeling expenses through a home business means that the business pays taxes (instead of the individual). This is not the case, however, channeling expenses through the business can **eliminate paying any taxes** on expenses.

Family Tax Benefits

To reduce your personal tax bill even further, you can pay more money to your partner and reduce the amount you pay to yourself, thus putting yourself on a lower tax bracket. You can also pay your children from the business, tax-free.

Different countries have different tax rules on child payments, but some countries allow you to pay around $5,000, tax-free, to children from out of a business. That equals $10,000 of tax-free money every year if you have two children.

If your children want to work in the business, there are many tasks they can do, depending on their age. Internet business tasks include picking stock, packing, printing invoices, printing labels, filing, record keeping, Internet research, taking stock inventory, collapsing packing boxes, emptying bins, unpacking new stock, photography, re-packing stock after photography, and testing any items which may have been returned.

If you are not putting every expense that you legally can through your home business, you are more than likely paying way too much in taxes.

Depreciation

Items such as desktop computers, notebook computers, iPads, printers, routers, fax machines, (etc.) can be depreciated over a time interval of around 2-3 years – again, all countries have different rules and time frames. After this period, you can purchase new equipment and start the depreciation schedule again. This is a good way of getting a new computer, and continuously increasing the numbers of computers in your house for the kids as well as new staff members; and all tax-free.

Health Insurance

In countries like the United States where there is no government-funded health insurance, you can set up a health insurance account to pay staff health insurance. This is another huge tax benefit from running a home business. Again, talk to your accountant about this.

A Final Note on Taxes

Think of every $1,000 of tax that you are not required to pay as a $1,000 pay rise.

There are many more tax reasons to claim all of your expenses through your business, and of course, every country is different. This is only written as an overview: you should always consult your accountant for tax advice, as tax rules are different in every country. Of course, you can even pay for your accountant through your business!

It amazes me how many of my students get caught up in not wanting to pay taxes. The goal should always be to claim every expense legally possible in order to pay for as much tax as possible! The person who pays the most tax after claiming every possible expense is normally making the most money!

CHAPTER FIVE

Opening an eBay Account

*"If we are facing in the right direction,
all we have to do is keep on walking."*

~ BUDDHIST PROVERB ~

Opening an eBay account is simple and it's free!

First, choose a URL from below for the country in which you are located:

ASIA

Australia:	www.eBay.com.au
Hong Kong:	www.eBay.com.hk
India:	www.eBay.com.in
Malaysia:	www.eBay.com.my
New Zealand:	www.eBay.co.nz
Philippines:	www.eBay.ph
Singapore:	www.eBay.sg
South Korea:	www.eBay.co.kr

EUROPE

Austria:	www.eBay.at
Belgium:	www.eBay.be
France:	www.eBay.fr
Germany:	www.eBay.de
Ireland:	www.eBay.ie
Italy:	www.eBay.it
Netherlands:	www.eBay.nl
Poland:	www.eBay.pl
Spain:	www.eBay.es
Sweden:	www.eBay.se
Switzerland:	www.eBay.ch
United Kingdom:	www.eBay.co.uk

NORTH AMERICA

Canada:	www.eBay.ca
America:	www.eBay.com

For this example, I will use eBay America, which is www.eBay.com

To create an account with eBay, simply click on the "register" button, which, per the picture below, is located at the top of the eBay home page. Then simply enter your details.

By opening an account in your country, you are not restricting yourself to only selling items within your country. eBay has made the borders between countries transparent, meaning that buyers in all countries can find you, no matter what country you are located in. You will, however, always find the most competitive shipping prices to customers in your own country. It is cheaper for you to mail items domestically to, say, your next door neighbor, than it would be for someone from another country to send the same item to your next door neighbor.

On average, 9% of sales from our Australian eBay businesses are from overseas buyers, even though it costs a fortune to send items from Australia to Europe or the United States (due to geographical distance). Despite this reality, 9% of buyers are still happy to pay the international postage.

I highly recommend that you concentrate on selling within your own country, treating international sales as a bonus, and you will get them. Setting up inventory in other countries to increase the size of your business is a lot harder than simply adding more products to your existing business!

Password

Make sure you create a password which is harder than average to crack. Combine upper and lower case letters and numbers (e.g., 5Password812. Don't use obvious numbers (like your birthday or your driver's license number).

Choosing a User ID

eBay allows you to choose your own eBay user ID. All eBay ID's must have no spaces.

Note: Your eBay ID is visible to buyers. Try to think up a user ID which sounds trustworthy and is suitable for a million dollar eBay business. Don't use a silly or bizarre name: it will stop people buying from you.

If you already have an eBay account, you can change your existing ID, but you can only change it once every 30 days. To change your eBay ID, click on the "My eBay" link, located at the top of most eBay pages; then click the "Account" tab and scroll down to the "Personal Information" link. Lastly, click the "Edit" link to the very right, on the same line as "User ID."

PayPal

After setting up your eBay account, eBay encourages sellers to set up a PayPal account. Guess who owns PayPal? Yep: eBay. I have been to many seminars where people whinge and moan about PayPal. Personally, I love PayPal. It is by far the most popular way that buyers pay for purchases on eBay, and it works worldwide. Yes, they charge for their services, but in my view, the person who pays the most in PayPal fees is, again, normally making the most money!

Why PayPal? As PayPal's website says, PayPal is fast, safe and secure. It is better for buyers than credit cards, as PayPal provides buyer protection if the buyer never receives the item, or if the item differs from its description on eBay. It is also better for sellers, as it affords more protection than a credit card, due to PayPal security checks. Many eBay buyers will only purchase from sellers who accept PayPal due to the buyer protection that PayPal provides.

If a customer purchases an item through eBay and it never arrives, or it is significantly different from how it was described by the seller, PayPal will reimburse the buyer for up to $20,000. This gives the buyer peace of mind, which gives you more sales.

PayPal Buyer Protection Rules:

- PayPal "Buyer Protection" excludes bikes, cars, boats, and other vehicles, services, and real estate.
- Transactions must be completed solely on eBay, directly with the seller.
- PayPal must be used to pay for the item.
- Items must be physically tangible.
- Complaints must be lodged within 45 days of payment.

PayPal Fees

At the time of writing, the fees below applied for Australia, however, check with PayPal in your country to confirm the amounts that PayPal charges in your country.

Purchase Payments Received (Monthly, Base Rate)	Fee Per Transaction
$0 AUD - $5,000 AUD	2.4% + $0.30 AUD
$5,000 AUD - $15,000 AUD	2.0% + $0.30 AUD
$15,000 AUD - $150,000 AUD	1.5`% + $0.30 AUD
> $150,000.00 AUD	1.1% + $0.30 AUD

The standard rate for receiving payments is 2.4%.

If you receive more than $3,000 per month, you're eligible to apply for a Merchant Rate, which lowers your fees as your sales volume increases. Your fees can be as low as 1.1%, based on your previous month's sales volume.

As soon as you hit $3,000 apply for the PayPal Merchant Account.

You can also accept checks, money orders, bank transfers and credit card payments, but PayPal is the most popular method, and many large sellers only accept PayPal. If you decide to set up a PayPal account, use a different password from your eBay account.

Having a PayPal account also allows you to send money to anyone else's PayPal account, even if they are in a different country, as PayPal exists in most countries.

In some countries, eBay even offers a debit/credit card which you can use at an ATM to withdraw funds straight from your PayPal account.

PayPal Virtual Terminal

PayPal's "virtual terminal" is another service that PayPal offers to merchants. It allows you to accept credit card payments over the phone, by mail, or by fax.

eBay PowerSeller

Once you have completed a minimum of 100 transactions and $3,000 USD in sales over a period of 12 months, and you meet the requirements below, you will automatically become an eBay "PowerSeller." There is no charge for PowerSeller status.

PowerSeller Criteria:

- Must be registered with eBay for a minimum of 90 days.
- Must have an account in good standing (i.e., you are up-to-date on any eBay transaction fees).
- Must maintain a positive feedback rating of 98% or greater over a period of 12 months.
- Must abide by eBay policies (e.g., not selling counterfeit products).
- Must have made a minimum of 100 transactions and $3,000 USD in sales over a period of 12 months.
- Must receive at least a 4.40 average from buyers across all four categories of seller ratings (DSR's).
- Must have no more than 1.00% of transactions with low DSR's (1's or 2's) on "Item as described," and no more than 2.00% of low DSR's on "Communication," "Postage time," and "Postage and handling cost."
- No violation of any severe policies (e.g., "Shill Bidding") in the last 60 days.

The Benefits of Becoming a PowerSeller

- Priority telephone support.
- Priority email support.
- PowerSeller "best practice" discussion board.
- Quarterly newsletters.
- Automatic display of " PowerSeller" next to your user ID.

As a PowerSeller, you also have the opportunity to qualify for "Top Rated seller status," which recognizes merchants who have a proven track record of excellent customer service and sales. Sellers with Top Rated seller status have their listings shown 33% more than sellers who do not have Top Rated seller status.

There are 5 different levels of PowerSeller:

PowerSeller Level	Min. Sales (12 mo.)	Min. Transactions
Bronze	$3,000 USD	100
Silver	$36,000 USD	3,600
Gold	$120,000 USD	12,000
Platinum	$300,000 USD	30,000
Titanium	$1,800,000 USD	180,000

When you get to "Platinum" and "Titanium" status, you will receive your own eBay account manager.

The "About Me" Page

The "About Me" page is where you can tell customers a little bit about yourself and/or your company. You can also upload a photo of yourself to show some personality. It is also the ONLY place where you are allowed to post a URL (e.g., www.whatever.com) that links to your non-eBay store (if you have one).

Your "About Me" page lets customers know that you are someone who cares about his or her customers, and that you are passionate about the products you sell. Don't tell customers how wonderful you and your company are as they don't care. They just want to know that you care about them and that they are not going to get ripped off!

Also, don't threaten potential buyers with all of the things you are prepared to do to customers who don't pay, or who leave you negative feedback. Remember, like attracts like. If you discuss negative things in your "About Me" page, you will not only lose good customers, but you will also attract negative, aggressive ones.

If you show people that you value their business, it will encourage them to work with you if they have any problems later on.

To get to the "About Me" page, click on "Site Map," which is at the bottom of every eBay page. Then, in the third column, click on the "About Me" link.

Gaining Feedback

Every time you buy and sell something on eBay, you have an opportunity to leave feedback. If you are new to eBay, instead of making purchases at your local stores, practice channelling some of your purchases through eBay. This includes printer ink, clothing, shoes, toys, hobbies, computer software, books, packing boxes, tape dispensers, gifts, etc.

By purchasing through eBay, you will almost always save money as products are, on the whole, less expensive on eBay. You will also save gas and time from not having to drive to the store, because all of the items will be delivered to your front door.

More importantly, you will increase your feedback score with every purchase. You will also gain valuable experience, because you will be able to see how eBay works from a buyer's perspective.

For instance, when you are buying, take your time to observe the whole process carefully. What do you like about a seller? What annoys you? Do you like their photos? Do you like their ad copy? Do you like their terms and conditions? Can you sense that the seller is kind, and reasonable to deal with, or do you feel that the seller is arrogant and pushy? Read any emails you receive from a seller. Become familiar with every step of the process, every time you purchase anything. Take notes of everything you like and don't like. Taking this time to monitor your preferences about other sellers will quickly propel you into the mindset of a Top Rated eBay salesperson.

Once your eBay account has ten or more feedback ratings, open another eBay account, and channel all your future *purchases* through that account. Use the one with the highest feedback rating to *sell* items. By doing this, you will always have a spare eBay account with 100% feedback **as sellers can only leave positive feedback**.

Note: There is no difference on eBay for feedback received from selling something or from buying something. It does not matter if you get your ratings from selling ten pairs of old shoes or from buying ten baseball cards: ten feedbacks are ten feedbacks!

The secret to feedback is to get to ten as fast as possible, because when a buyer sees ten or more feedbacks, it makes the seller look more trustworthy.

One of my students recently purchased ten stamps to get ten speedy feedbacks; then turned around and resold them to get ten more!

This is a very aggressive way of buying feedback, and is not required. We have never had to do this. (More on feedback in Chapter 8).

eBay Rules

There are many eBay rules and regulations. Most are common sense, so I am just going to list the ones which I get asked about the most. If you break these rules, eBay will close your listings and can also suspend and even ban you from eBay. (Banning is usually reserved for repeat offenders).

Shill Bidding

"Shill bidding" means bidding on your own auctions. This is a very big no, no. Neither you, your family members, your work colleagues nor your friends are allowed to bid on any of your eBay auctions! If you think that eBay will not find out, I highly recommend you think again.

Years ago, my brother-in-law innocently bid on a $20 item we were selling, and the next thing I knew, our listings had all been suspended. We were required to take an online course on "shill bidding," and we had to face a bright, red "Policy Violation" in our eBay dashboard, warning us at all times that if it happened again, we could be permanently suspended. We did not ask our relative to bid on this item; he just liked it, and wanted it. We had absolutely no idea that he placed a bid, yet this $20 item could have closed our million dollar eBay account.

Note: Family, friends, and co-workers *can* buy goods from your eBay store, but only if the item is being sold with a *fixed price.*

Posting URL's in Listings

The only place that eBay allows you to include URL's (e.g., www.xyz. com) is in your "About Me" page. You cannot get around this rule by writing the URL out (e.g., "for more information, see xyz dot com"), or by using any other similar trick, either.

TKO Warnings

You get a TKO (or "takeover") warning if you sell trademarked items and the owner of the trademark contacts eBay to report you for selling a counterfeit product (i.e., a "Gucci" bag or a "Rolex" watch). TKO warnings are why we do not like to sell any new products that have brand names.

Fee Circumvention

Fee circumvention occurs when a buyer deliberately uses eBay to find customers, but then conducts sales outside of eBay, circumventing eBay's "final value" fee. For example, some buyers choose to list items on the auction format, and then sell these items for cash to someone who contacts them through eBay. The seller then closes the auction early.

When this happens, eBay only receives its listing fee, but not its final value fee. This is unfair to eBay, as they have generated the machine which located the buyer, so it is only fair they should get paid for their service. Anyone who attempts fee circumvention is building a business on quicksand, because if and when they get caught, eBay can either suspend or terminate their account.

Getting Help

eBay has a very comprehensive self-help section which can be accessed by clicking on the "Customer Service" button, located at the top, right-hand side of every eBay page.

Normally, you can find the answers to most of your questions, but if you have an elaborate one, or you feel that you need to communicate with an eBay representative directly, you can find the necessary contact information on the Customer service page.

CHAPTER SIX

Listing a Product

"The cave you fear to enter holds the treasure you seek."

~ Joseph Campbell ~

To list an item on eBay, click on the "Sell" button, as per the screen-shot below:

You will then get a box similar to the one below:

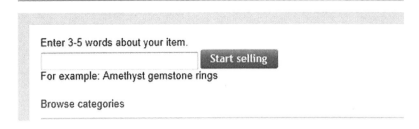

Enter a basic keyword(s) about your item (e.g., "gnome"). Remember; don't use too many keywords, as more keywords equal less search results. Perhaps one keyword might work?

I typed in "gnome" and got the following:

Find a matching category

Enter 3-5 words about your item.

gnome   [Search]

For example: Nine West women's shoes

| Suggested categories | Select a suitable category |

Buyers will see your listing in the category that you select.

Home & Garden
- ☐ Gardening > Décor, Furnishing > Sculpture, Statues
- ☐ Home Décor > Figurines
- ☐ Wedding Supplies > Favours > Other Favours
- ☐ Parties, Occasions > Favours

Collectables
- ☐ Fantasy, Magic > Gnomes

Books, Magazines
- ☐ Children's Books

Now, check the box which suits your product. For this one, I checked "Gardening > Décor, Furnishing > Sculpture, Statues."

If you are listing a new item using the profit strategies in the previous chapters, it is important to list the item in the exact same category, as you know that it sells well there.

To find out which category an item is listed under, find the item in eBay using the example below:

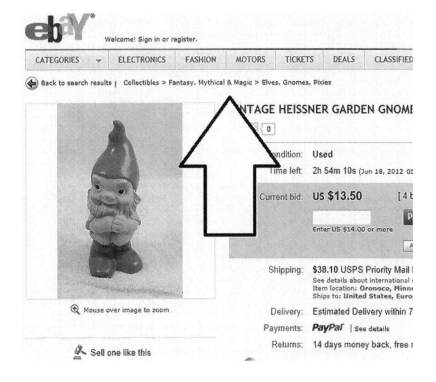

In the example above, you can see the category is "Collectables > Fantasy, Mythical & Magic > Elves, Gnomes, Pixies."

Select whichever category is correct for your item.

eBay will then give you the opportunity to run your ad in a second category for an extra fee. We only ever list in one category, because we run tests to determine which category produced the most sales (per the previous chapters). We then keep listing the item in the single, most successful category.

Keywords

Keywords are critical: Select the wrong keywords for your title and your item becomes a needle in a haystack. The good news is, it is easy to select the keywords which attract the most buyers to your item.

Previously, eBay allowed us to use 55 characters in the title, but now they have upped it to 80 characters per title. The title is where you must include the best, *most relevant* keywords to get the most traffic to your item. Every good, relevant keyword brings more potential buyers to your listing. Every non-relevant keyword is a waste of time. Simply using 40 characters potentially halves the amount of buyers who will find your listing; try to use as many of the 80 characters as possible. Remember: Keep it relevant.

For example, recently I was involved in the purchase of a used aluminum boat for a friend on eBay. By scrolling through the categories instead of typing keywords into the eBay search box, we found a boat that was up for auction with the title "Quintrex Dory 420 for sale." This is a classic example of using irrelevant keywords. What about using some keywords like "boat"???

Only a very small amount of buyers could have known what a "Quintrex Dory 420" was. For everyone else typing basic words like "boat" or "aluminum boat" into the search box, this ad would not have come up in the search results. For the ones in the know, "Quintrex" is a boat manufacturer and the "Dory 420" is a model. For everyone else, this boat was invisible (unless they trawled through every boat listing manually, like we did).

Most people type words like "aluminum boat," "dinghy," "trailer boat," (etc.). Had the ad read "Quintrex Dory 420 Aluminum Trailer Dinghy Fishing Boat," then it would have been visible to over 50 times more viewers!

To make matters worse, the seller had listed it for a seven-day auction beginning on a Saturday at 1:30 a.m. Consequently, when the auction finished seven days later at 1:30 in the morning, everyone was asleep!

Yep, we ended up buying the boat for a song!

To find the correct, most relevant keywords for your item, make a list of what you think the best keywords are and THEN have a look at which keywords the TOP selling similar items use.

Make sure you use all of the 80 characters eBay allows. Don't shortchange yourself with only using, say, 50 characters - every keyword sends more viewers to your item.

The order of the keywords in the title does not affect the eBay search algorithm, but it does sound better to your buyers if your keywords are in some sort of flowing order. Always try to make your ads flow like a poem. Which sounds better: "New porcelain garden gnome," or "Garden porcelain gnome new?" The eBay search robot may not care, but the buyers do.

Make sure if the item does have a brand name and/or model number that you include these. For example, if you were selling a Canon camera with a model number of IXUS 100, you would include these keywords: "Canon IXUS 100 Camera." If an item is new, add the keyword "New" at the beginning of the title, as buyers often use the word "new" when searching for things (e.g., "new black T-shirt." Don't write "Brand new," as "brand" is a waste of five of your 80 characters: buyers do not use the word "brand" when searching for items. If the item you are selling is old, consider using the keywords "Antique" or "Vintage."

For some items, such as clothing, mobile phone accessories, etc., include the color as a keyword in your title. This works with most items that come in various colors.

Using words like "and," "is," "for," "attractive," "L@@k," "****," etc., is a waste of characters, as buyers do not type these words into the search bar. Just use relevant keywords, and make sure that you've spelled them correctly: a misspelled keyword will not get the same amount of traffic as one that is spelled correctly.

Always separate your keywords with a space - never with punctuation. If you type "Canon!" (with the exclamation point) and a buyer searches "Canon" (without the exclamation point), your listing will not show up in their search results. It will only show up if a buyer searches "Canon!" Don't hold your breath waiting for somebody to do a search for that.

Over time, sellers have created eBay acronyms which they use in the title, but I think these are an absolute waste of space – literally – as only some of the sellers and very seasoned buyers know what they mean! Every time we test them, we get less traffic, and hence, lower sales.

For your reference, here is the list of popular eBay acronyms:

- 1st First Edition (used in book titles).
- ANTH   Anthology (used in book titles).
- AUTO   Autographed.
- BOMC   Book of the Month Club Edition (used in book titles).
- COA   Certificate of Authenticity.
- COL   Collection.
- FS   Free Shipping.
- GBP   Great Britain Pounds.
- HB   Hardbound (used in book titles).
- HB/DJ   Hardbound with Dust Jacket.
- HTF   Hard to Find (come on, honestly, how many buyers would work that out?)
- LTD   Limited Edition.
- MIB   Mint in Box.
- MIJ   Made in Japan.
- MOC   Mint on Card.
- NBW   Never Been Worn.
- NC   No Cover (used in book titles).
- NIB   New in Box.
- NM   Near Mint.
- NEW   New Old Stock (what the . . ?).
- NR   Can mean No Reserve or Not Real.
- NWOT   New Without Tags.
- NWT   New With Tags.

- OEM   Original Equipment Manufacturer.
- OOAK   One of a Kind.
- OOP   Out of Print (used in book titles).
- PB   Paperback (used in book titles).
- SH   Shipping and Handling.
- VHTF   Very Hard to Find (and very hard to work out the acronym)!

Always remember, *every relevant* keyword in the title will bring more traffic. The more relevant keywords you have, the more traffic your listing will get.

For used items, there is no need to guess what the best keywords are; just look at the "completed listings" for similar products, and see which keywords the sellers used.

Another way to get the best keywords is through Google. If you search for anything on Google, you will find the top eight similar searches at the very bottom of your search results.

For example, I typed "log splitter" into the search bar, (below):

Whitlands Engineering
www.superaxe.com.au/
Whitlands Engineering is Australia's leading specialist manufacturer of Firewood Processors and Wood Splitters for all commercial, semi-commercial, farm and ....

LOG SPLITTERS Sherwood Machinery Pty Ltd Product Range
www.sherwoodmachinery.com.au/products/logsplitters.html
The Sherwood log splitter range allows for the splitting of firewood logs up to 20" long (500 mm) with a splitting force of up to 20 tons, using a 4" bore cylinder, ...

Our 2012 logsplitter line-up revealed - Parklands Power Products ...
www.parklands.net/blog/Our-2012-logsplitter-line-up-revealed
14 May 2012 – Warm your home with wood split by Parklander log splitters 14-05-2012...

Searches related to **log splitter**

log splitter for sale	log splitter hire
log splitter reviews	masport log splitter
used hydraulic log splitter	hydraulic log splitter
log splitter plans	hydraulic log splitter plans

Goooooooooogle ›

1 2 3 4 5 6 7 8 9 10   Next

Advanced search   Search Help   Give us feedback   Go to Google.com

Google Home   Advertising Programmes   Business Solutions   Privacy & Terms   About Google

From the results here, I can see that "hydraulic" is a hot keyword. You can then add the word "hydraulic" to your search to find out what other keywords people are searching on.

Using the correct keywords is the crucial element in bringing traffic to your listings.

Subtitles

After you complete the title, your next entry is the "Subtitle." These are useful for selling more expensive items, but they are too expensive for a $5 item! On the Australian eBay site, it costs $2 to include a subtitle. When we choose to use them (for more expensive items), we usually include phrases like, "Australian Seller," "Free Shipping," etc. Again, check out the competition for your product. You can also check out eBay sellers in other countries to see what phrases they are using (e.g., Canada, USA, UK, etc.).

Note: eBay searches *do not* take into account any keywords you include in the subtitle:

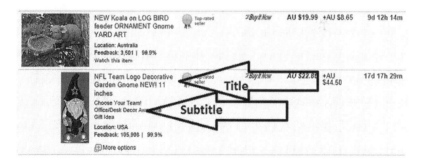

Item Specifics

The "Item Specifics" field lets you provide details ("specs") about an item you're selling, such as the brand, size, make, model, color, style, etc. These details appear in a consistent format at the top of your listing description, making it easy for buyers to get the facts about your item.

Note: The option to include item specifications is not available for all categories, but eBay is continually adding the Item Specifics option for other categories.

This is how it works. Take the Motor Vehicle Accessories category, for example. eBay's goal for this category is to let a buyer quickly find any part for almost any car. Let's say you need a radiator cap for a Ford Mustang. Using the Item Specifics field, the buyer can go to eBay, select "Motors," then "Parts and Accessories," type in "radiator cap," click on "Ford," then "Mustang," and Bingo! Up comes radiator caps - ONLY for a Ford Mustang.

The process is fast and simple.

Item specifics works the same way for other items, like shoes, in that you can easily narrow your search down to "leather boys shoes size 7," and you will only see boys' leather shoes in size 7. Same with fashion: you can quickly narrow the search down to find exactly what you want. Recently, I wanted to buy some black mens plain T-shirts made from cotton in size XXL. Using the Item Specifics field, I was able to quickly narrow my search down in order to find the exact shirt I was after. Two days later, it arrived at my front door!

Remember, not every category gives you the "Item Specifics" option, but if your category does, make sure you use it!

Your next step in advertising is to add pictures.

Add Pictures

eBay now allows sellers to upload up to twelve pictures for free, largely due to the phenomenal success of the eBay app on smartphones and iPads. In the past, we would create our eBay ads using an HTML program (like Dreamweaver), thus loading our pictures into external software. If you use this method, your pictures will not show up in the images section of the eBay app for buyers who use smartphones and iPads. You now must load all the pictures directly onto eBay.com for the pictures to display in the images section of the eBay app.

Take pictures of as many "features and benefits" as possible, in order to proactively answer as many of your buyers' questions as possible. Remember the saying: "A picture speaks a thousand words," or in eBay's case, "A picture answers a thousand questions!"

Gallery Pictures

Gallery pictures are critical: they are the first images a buyer sees when they search for an item on eBay. You will get five times more clicks on your item if you include a gallery picture.

Once you have uploaded your gallery picture, your next step is to complete the "Describe" field. As it says, this is where we describe what we are selling.

First, write a short one or two paragraph sales pitch about the item. If you are not good at thinking up narratives, look at the other people's listings and/or magazine/website advertisements for inspiration on the same/similar products.

Next, jot down as many features and benefits as possible. Write as many as you can think of, and then check the supplier's website for more. Most importantly, **check the "Completed Listings" for which features and benefits are being listed for similar items that have had the best previous sales on eBay** (as per Chapter 3).

What is the difference between a feature and a benefit?

A kitchen knife might be advertised as using 440 stainless steel. To figure out the difference between a feature and a benefit, ask yourself the "So what?" question (i.e., "So what if it has 440 stainless? What does that mean? What benefit does that give me?").

Benefits are the key to getting people excited; features put people to sleep. I'm no stainless expert, but a quick Google tells me 440 stainless is harder than 300 stainless. Now that's a benefit. Yes, I would prefer a harder knife than a softer one!

A garden gnome might be painted with XYZ paint (a feature), but again, who cares! Its benefit is that the paint doesn't fade for 10 years in your garden: now that "benefit" - not fading - interests me.

Try to convert all the "features" into benefits for the buyers.

A couple of years ago, I went bicycle shopping with my two sons. We went to a local bike shop and were quickly helped by an enthusiastic young sales assistant who couldn't have been more than 16 years of age. I will never forget this young mans natural ability to point out all the "benefits" of the more expensive bikes. I remember how he pointed out how certain parts of the frame were inserted further into the frame (a feature) on the more expensive bikes than the cheaper ones. The "benefit," as the young salesman quickly pointed out, was that the frame joins were much stronger and could withstand much larger jumps. If he had just said, "These frames are stronger" on the more expensive model, I probably would not have believed him, but he pointed out why. Needless to say, I walked out with two bikes which cost double the amount I originally had in mind. Because of this, I had to go home and point out all the "benefits" to my wife so I could justify why I spent so much!

Bottom line: if your item has it, POINT THE "BENEFIT" OUT, using strategic text and images. Never, ever assume that your customer will know that your product has certain features or benefits - always point it out.

Bullet Points

- This is a bullet point (i.e., the little black dot to the left of this sentence).
- List as many features and benefits as possible in bullet form. Features and benefits sell BIG time. List as many as possible.

WARNING: The average ratio of questions to items listed on eBay is two (i.e., two questions for every item listed, per day).

If you do not want to be bombarded with email questions, try to answer every single question on your ad copy, using text and images. If you list an item and are continually asked the same question(s), go back to eBay and modify your ad copy to include the answer to the question(s).

Urgency

Try to put something in your listing to create a sense of urgency - a reason why the potential buyer needs to purchase or bid now!

We use the following phrases:

- Limited Stock.
- Only "X" available - then they are all gone.
- End-of-Season Sale.
- Winter/Summer/Spring/Autumn/Fall Sale.
- Brand New Model - Just Arrived - Limited Stock.
- Rare.
- Unique.

Ownership

The feeling of ownership for bidders works well in auctions. This sense of ownership before the auction is over is what drives the high auction prices.

We use phrases like:

- How will you feel when your partner sees you are wearing the XYZ?
- How will you feel wearing the XYZ?
- The XYZ will look stunning in your XYZ.

If you can get them to visualize the item on their body, or in their house, car, garden, etc., then your job is done. The buyer can then switch from their logical brain at auction time to their irrational brain, which places high bids.

Terms and Conditions

We put our terms and conditions at the bottom of each listing.

Keep these as simple as possible, and try to be as positive as possible. Do not threaten potential buyers with negative phrases like, "If you do not pay within 2 days, then we will re-list the item and leave you negative feedback."

Who wants to buy from someone who is that arrogant?

List the types of payment you accept (e.g., PayPal, money orders, direct bank deposit, bank checks, personal checks, cashier's checks, etc.). If you accept personal checks, make sure you state that you will not ship until after the check has cleared.

What is your Warranty and Return policy?

Do you offer local pick-up? If you do/do not, document it in your terms and conditions.

Personally, we never offer customer pick-up, as it can be a nightmare for the following four reasons:

1. Customers often want pick-up items to be delivered after work hours, and we do not want to work during non-business hours.

2. Say a customer says he or she will arrive at 2 p.m. on a Saturday afternoon, so you stay home. Then the customer calls at 2 p.m. to say they are running late because of XYZ, and they will arrive at 3 p.m. instead. The customer finally arrives – late - at 3:20 p.m., and would like to see a demonstration of the item before purchasing. The customer ultimately likes the item but forgot to go to an ATM on the way over. The customer goes to an ATM and returns 30 minutes later to pay you for the item. At 4:40 p.m. you wave them goodbye, and suddenly realize you have lost Saturday afternoon with your family for a profit of $23! This might sound far-fetched but it is a true story.

3. The buyer now knows where you live and may feel like driving over to claim a warranty on a Sunday evening, un-announced!

4. The customer usually receives your landline or mobile number to assist in arranging pickup time. Many customers do not understand you run a business which, like other businesses, has office hours (refer back to point #1). A phone call at 9 p.m. on Sunday night for a "quick question" is not my idea of office hours, but many buyers disagree.

Pick-ups are okay for large, expensive items (like a boat), however the huge amount of time that they take makes them unprofitable for small, and lower cost items.

Warranty

Here is a scary subject for most eBay newbies, but it really isn't that bad.

We always offer long warranties (12 months) as it offers potential buyers peace of mind. We have been doing this for nearly 10 years, so we have some pretty good data to rely on.

The reality is most item failures happen within the first few weeks, so if you offered a 30-day warranty, it would hardly make any difference. In fact, because eBay customers can leave negative feedback for 60 days from the date of purchase, sellers tend to bend over backwards to keep customers happy during the 60 days, regardless of whatever warranty they offer.

After two months, warranty claims drop right off. If you do receive any warranty claims after two months, make sure you tell the customer they MUST provide a copy of their invoice when they return the item as proof of purchase. (Many people do not keep receipts).

This may sound like we ask for invoices knowing that most people have lost them (which cut down on warranty repairs) and this is partly true, but on the other hand, we have had several items returned for warranty which were not even purchased from us!

What's more, you can ask for replacements from the manufacturers to replace warranty items that you have sold, and you can also sell returned items as used items to recoup more money.

Bottom line: Offering long warranties gets more sales.

Return Policy

Many sellers write "All sales are final," which, again, sounds arrogant, and certainly does not give a buyer the 'warm and fuzzies', nor does it make a buyer feel safe and secure. Instead, we write "We gladly accept returns for 30 days from purchase for any unopened items."

We rarely get any buyers sending back any unopened items, but if we do, we can easily re-list them and sell them again.

We also get the extra sales, as customers prefer this return policy to the "All sales are final!"

Smiley Face

Including a smiley face in your ad copy definitely changes the dynamic for someone reading your ad, and ultimately increases the sales price.

HTML or Text?

You can either write the description of the item with text, or you can use an HTML program (like Dreamweaver) and then paste in the HTML. If the word "HTML" sounds like alien space talk, then text is just fine. I'm continually blown away by how well basic text ads perform. Don't be fooled into thinking that a fancy ad will outperform a basic text ad. We have A/B split tested this over the years, literally thousands of times, with products and websites. Just because a page/site looks fancy DOES NOT mean it converts sales better. Never, ever ask for the opinion of a graphic artist UNLESS they have a lot of SPLIT testing sales conversion experience.

A/B testing - split testing - is a method of testing to see which ad (for the same item) gets the best response (or "conversion rate"). To clarify: "Ad A" might get 20 sales and "Ad B" might get 40 sales, so Ad B is the winner.

For new products (using the strategies outlined in Chapter 3), we already know which ads were the best performers: the ones which got the most sales!

Note: If you would like to learn how to use an HTML program like Dreamweaver, you can either buy a book (e.g., *Dreamweaver for Dummies*) or attend an evening course. In Australia, they hold evening courses at local community colleges, night schools, etc.) for all kinds of subjects (from sewing to computer courses), including Dreamweaver. The best way to find these is to contact your local city council or government library.

These evening courses normally run for three – six weeks, one night per week.

Spell Check

A listing with spelling and/or grammatical errors looks unprofessional and immediately makes the potential buyer lose confidence.

The more educated the buyer, the more they will lose confidence. If you are selling a used bicycle for teenagers, you can get away with spelling errors, but if you are selling a new "quality" item, spelling errors can dramatically affect sales.

Make sure you take the time to proofread all of your listings. If you are not the greatest speller, you can copy your listings into a program like Microsoft Word and then run the Spelling & Grammar check. You can then paste it back into eBay.

Listing Types and Times

- Auction.
- Auction with a BIN (Buy It Now) option.
- Classifieds.
- eBay Stores (see Chapter 9: Opening an eBay Store).
- Fixed Price (Buy it Now).
- Reserves and Best Offer.

We only use Auction, Auction with BIN, Best Offer and eBay Stores.

Auction

The best time to finish auctions for most products is around 9 p.m. on Sunday night. All other nights are okay, but not as good as Sunday night. The exception is Friday night, which is normally the worst. Three-day auctions are the best bang for your buck, but seven- and ten-day auctions will normally get a slightly higher price, due to the fact that they attract more "watchers" over the course of seven days. However, you will make fewer sales due to the fact that it takes seven to ten days. Some HOT items will work on auction, whereas others may not. The items which work best on auction are items with a strong demand.

Note: In a country like the USA where there are different time zones (i.e., 9 p.m. in New York and 6 p.m. in California) it is nor-mally best to list the item halfway in-between (i.e., 7:30 pm PST). However, some items sell better on the east coast than the west coast, so you need to either experiment with times or study the other top sellers of the product you are selling.

The only exception for ending an auction on a Sunday night is when there is a huge event on TV, like a major football game.

eBay is slowly moving away from auction format in favor of BIN (Buy It Now), so we rarely use auctions now. I believe auction will still be offered on eBay for a long time, but that it will mostly be used for second-hand items.

If you list an item for auction, always consider what people may be doing when your auction finishes. For instance, at 3 p.m., most moms are picking up the kids, and at 5:30 p.m. most people are driving home: they are not in front of their computers.

In the past, we always started auctions at the lowest price possible, with no reserve (e.g., at 99 cents). This scares a lot of people but it works for most items, due to the psychological reason of "ownership." To elaborate: When a person is winning an auction, they feel like the item is theirs. Very often, their ego takes over. I could write a book on the reasons behind auction mentality, but for now, just take my word for it - or even better, test it yourself and watch the competition.

Note: The closer the time is to the end of your auction, the more traffic your listing will get. This is because eBay will only show your listing on the *first* page of the search results during the *last* few hours.

Auction with BIN

This is the same as auction-style listing, but you list the item with a BIN price as well, so if a buyer wants it right then and there, they can purchase it immediately (thus ending the auction).

Note: If any buyer bids on the item, the BIN option disappears.

The Buy it Now price also comes with an added bonus for your auction: it helps set the perceived value of your item.

Buy it Now (BIN)

As the name suggests, this is when you list an item for a fixed price. The advantage of using BIN is that you only pay the listing fee once per listing, even if you are listing 20 pieces of the same item. If you choose to auction your merchandise, you will have to pay a listing fee for every item.

Classified Ads

We do not use classified ads. Classifieds on eBay work the same way as placing ads in your local paper, however, on eBay, you are not restricted to the amount of words you use (as you are when you place newspaper ads).

Classified ads on eBay are used to sell cars, boats, caravans and services. In contrast with normal eBay listings, classified ads include your personal contact information (typically, your phone number) so that you can communicate directly with buyers.

Good Til Cancelled (GTC)

If you have an eBay store (see Chapter 9 for more information), you can list your items as "Good Til Cancelled" (GTC). With GTC, your listing will be posted for a duration of 30 days. At the end of the 30-day period, your listing will be automatically renewed and relisted. This continues to happen after every 30-day period until such time that the seller cancels the listing. Choosing GTC radically cuts down on listing fees because you can list 10 or 100 of the same item and only ever pay one listing fee.

People often confuse a GTC listing with a "Fixed Price, 30-day" listing. While most of the features are similar for both GTC and Fixed Price listings, the one big difference is that a Fixed Price, 30-day listing will close completely after 30 days, and all sales history will be deleted; whereas a GTC listing will be renewed, preserving the sales history.

The main benefit of a GTC listing is that sellers who have high inventories of the same products can keep a listing going on until they have sold all of their stock. They need not bother to create a new listing over and over again.

Another advantage of GTC listings is that previous sales history is carried forward in renewed GTC listings, and this helps the listing to appear higher in the results pages.

eBay is very fair when it comes to showing different sellers' ads. The eBay "Search" algorithm will always rotate ads to ensure that everybody gets a fair shot at selling their items; however, as time goes on, and the algorithm collects more sales history, the best performing listings will be displayed more often than the others. To get to the top of the search results, the eBay algorithm takes many factors into account, including the past sales history of your listing, your feedback rating, DSR's (more on DSR's in Chapter 7), Top-seller rating (or lack thereof), your listing price (including shipping), etc. The good news is, when you start, if your price is reasonably competitive, you can easily get onto the first page of the search results! eBay likes to encourage new sellers.

Reserve Price

Reserve prices pertain to auction listings. The reserve price is the lowest price that you will accept for an item.

Note: Reserve only works with certain items, like cars and boats. It does not work with the items we sell.

Best Offers

If you choose the "Accept Best Offers" option, you can list your item for sale on GTC for say, $100, and each buyer can forward you up to three offers. "Best Offer" works, but you will receive both good and crazy offers (i.e., people will offer you $5 for your $100 item; however there are others who will enter reasonable offers). You will receive these offers by email from eBay, and you can decide whether to accept or decline them. The good thing about best offers is that you can display a high price (e.g., $100), even though you are willing to accept lower prices. This keeps the market's "price perception" at $100, without encouraging a price war with another seller. Later on, you can program these "Best Offers" to be accepted and declined automatically.

Price

If you choose the BIN option, don't get into a price war - just sell at a similar price to the competition. Price wars normally become a battle of the egos, with your bank balance becoming the loser. You are better off using superior photos, more bullet points, kinder and friendlier terms and conditions, and including the most relevant item specifications.

Shipping

In many countries, eBay offers a free "Shipping Calculator." This is a great tool for buyers and sellers. Just describe your package's size and weight, enter whichever shipping services you want to use, and the shipping calculator will present the correct shipping cost to each buyer. That's all there is to it.

The next step is to find the lowest price for sending your items whilst enabling you to make some money on shipping. The best method is to go to your local post office with some of your merchandise and have a chat with them about the most cost-effective ways to send the items.

Let's say you list an item and elect to use eBay's built-in shipping calculator. Say the item sells for $100 and eBay automatically reports a shipping charge of $10 to the buyer. You can then ship the item for $5, making an extra $5 from the sale. This is well worth a trip to the post office.

When listing the item using the shipping calculator, if you increase the weight or the dimensions of the item, eBay charges the buyer a higher postage cost. Just be careful here: If you charge too much for postage, or charge more for postage than your competitors, it could come back to bite you when customers leave you poor feedback. You do need to cover your postage costs however. Packaging materials, time taken to go to the post office, fuel for your car, time taken to pack the item are all costs of sending your items that needs to be recouped in order to preserve your profit.

Buyers on eBay LOVE Free Shipping

If you can do local free shipping – do it. Obviously, nothing is for free (as you will have to pay for the postage), but just add the price of shipping into your sales price. If you offer "free" shipping, the eBay search algorithm will often bump your ad up higher, and you will get more traffic to your listing.

All countries have different methods of shipping, from independent couriers like Fedex, DHL, etc., to the more economical, government-owned postal systems.

In Australia, we use Australia Post for our local shipping and Australia Post Airmail for Internationals. Again, check to see what the competition is offering. In the U.S., Fedex is very popular for ground shipping, and U.S. mail is popular for international. All countries are different. For instance, in some countries, eBay allows you to set up different options for the buyers, from normal post to express. The buyer can then select which service they are willing to pay for.

International Shipping

I get many questions in regards to overseas shipping:

- "Should I?"
- "Shouldn't I?"
- "It takes too long because I have to fill out more paperwork. Is it really worth it?"
- "What if customers complain that the items take too long to ship, and they leave me negative feedback?"

Here is my response...

Firstly, we always ship internationally with all of our eBay accounts, however, you must:

1. Under-promise and over-deliver when quoting delivery times. To do this, contact whichever delivery service you plan to use and ask them how long it takes to mail items from your location to a variety of major geographical locations. Let's say you live in Florida, and you decide to use USPS for all of your international deliveries. Ask them how long it will take for delivery to Canada, Europe, Asia, Australia and the UK. If they say it will take, say, two weeks to Asia, write that the delivery time to Asia takes three weeks (i.e., 50% more time). This way, if a buyer gets it in two weeks and one day, they will be over the moon (instead of the reverse, if you had promised a two-week delivery in your listings).

2. Let customers know they are responsible for any and all local customs taxes and fees incurred in their own country.

3. State that you will not declare the items as a gift or write down that it is worth less than it is. Sure, you may lose a few sales, but you will also gain some, because customers will realize your business is ethical, and of high integrity. Don't come across as arrogant though: terms and conditions should sound fair, not arrogant.

Okay. That was the bad part about selling internationally. Here is the good stuff about international sales!

1. In Australia, we have a 10% GST (Goods and Services Tax) which is, as in most countries, only applicable to items that are used/consumed in the country. For every item that we sell internationally, we can claim that 10% back, which ultimately translates into an extra 10% profit on every international sale.
2. Higher auction prices: You only need two bidders at the end of an auction to push the price up. By opening up your listing to international buyers, you get more bidders.
3. More Sales! eBay now quotes that 20% of sales across the eBay platform are across borders.

Listing Upgrades That Make Your Listing Stand Out From the Crowd

When listing your items, eBay will offer optional listing upgrades, including "bold," "border," and "featured."

Bold

If you select "Bold," your 80-character title will show in bold. We use this on a lot of our items that sell for greater than $100, as it does make our listing stand out in the search results, however eBay does charge extra for it. In Australia, it costs $2, which is why we do not use it on items which sell for under $100. Of course, check what this fee is, in your own country.

In the screenshot below you can see the title (circled) which is in bold:

Bold is the only listing upgrade we use.

Border

The "border" upgrade literally puts a border around your listing when it is shown in the search results. The cost to include a border in Australia is $2.49.

Featured Plus

If you select "Featured Plus," your listing will show up in the top of the search results. Over the years, we have randomly tested "Featured Plus" on many different products; however we have rarely been able to make it pay for itself. The cost for using "Featured Plus" is $49.95.

Note: "Featured Plus" is only available to sellers with 10 or more feedbacks.

Gallery Featured

If you pay for the "Gallery Featured" option, your listing will periodically appear in the "Special Featured" section above the general gallery, and your picture will be nearly double the size of non-featured Gallery pictures. (Your listing will also appear in the general gallery). The cost for using "Gallery Featured" is $14.95.

Highlight

This option puts a background behind your listing in the search results to make it stand out. The cost to include a highlight is $3.00.

Home Page Featured (Single Quantity)

This is the exact wording from eBay:

> Your listing will have a chance to rotate into a special display on eBay's home page. Your item is very likely to show up on the home page, although eBay does not guarantee that your item will be highlighted in this way.

The bottom line is, if your listing *does* show on the home page, it will get a ton of extra viewers. This option only works if you have a product with mass market appeal, because buyers who are on the eBay Home page are almost certainly not looking for something other than the initial item that they are intending to purchase.

For the newbies out there wondering what a "home page" is: The homepage of any website is the first page you see when you enter a website. For example, when you type the URL "www. eBay.com" in your browser's address box and hit "return," the first page that appears is the eBay homepage. The cost of "Home Page Featured" is $49.95.

Home Page Featured (Multiple Quantity)

Same as above, except for when your listing has multiple quantities. The cost of "Home Page Featured (Multiple Quantity)" is $99.95.

Scheduled Listings

"Scheduled Listings" enables you to upload listings for auction but to start the auction at a later date and or time. This is critical if you cannot upload a listing at a desirable time (think back to the Quintrex boat example in the "Keywords" section in this chapter). We do not need to pay extra for the "scheduled listings" option as our auction management software automatically lists items at the times we set. (More on auction management software in Chapter 11: Automation). The cost for using "Scheduled Listings" is 20 cents.

A Final Note on Listing Upgrades

The bottom line is, we only use the "bold" option, as this is the only listing upgrade which we have tested that continually increases sales for us, but feel free to test the others yourself. Of course scheduled listings are also utilized by our software and I do highly recommend you use this upgrade to your advantage; it is well worth the extra 20 cents added to your listing fee.

While writing this chapter, I spent over an hour searching through different eBay listings, trying to find some that were using the upgrades detailed above so that I could get some screenshots for the book. I was unable to find any - the only ones I could find were for bold!

This leads to the assumption that other sellers are also not finding these listing upgrades very beneficial; otherwise, they would be using them.

Listing With Your Mobile Phone or iPad

If you choose to list items using eBay's smartphone/Ipad app, you can download it for free. These days, more and more items are listed using smartphones, however most of these items are used.

We do not use this app for listing any new items because we always use edited photos with the background removed, then upload them using desktop computers, and then list them using auction management software.

We *do* use the eBay app to sell our personal, used items, like bicycles. The app provides a very fast, simple way to list individual, used items. You just snap a picture of the item with your phone, and then use that same picture for your listing. Make sure you give it a go: its fun and its fast. According to eBay, you can create a listing in under one minute!

The eBay App is also a great tool to have on your mobile phone, because you can actively monitor how well all of your listings are performing. You will also receive alerts when an item sells. The eBay app allows you to: view how many items you have sold over the past 30 days, see and respond to "Best Offers," and respond to any questions you receive – anytime, anywhere!

We do almost all of our personal purchasing with the eBay app on an iPad. We prefer to search for items on the iPad over desktop computers, as the iPad allows users to view many more items at a time.

The eBay app allows you to:

- Purchase items anytime, anywhere, on your smartphone.
- Answer questions from buyers.
- Check your watched items.
- Research sales trends.
- List items.
- Scan barcodes of items to pre-populate your listing.
- Receive alerts if you are outbid, if a "watched item" ends, or if an auction ends.
- Compare prices while you are out shopping to prices on eBay using the barcode scanner (which uses the camera in

your phone). If the item is cheaper on eBay, you can pur-
chase it right then and there, before you leave the store!
- Upload photos from your phone to your eBay listing.
- View all of your eBay activity through "My eBay dashboard."
- Pay for purchases using PayPal.
- Share listings via email, Facebook, and Twitter.
- Leave feedback.

Keeping Track of What's Going On

The easiest way to keep track of what's going on with your
business is by clicking on "My eBay" for an account summary,
using your personal computer, laptop, smartphone or iPad device.

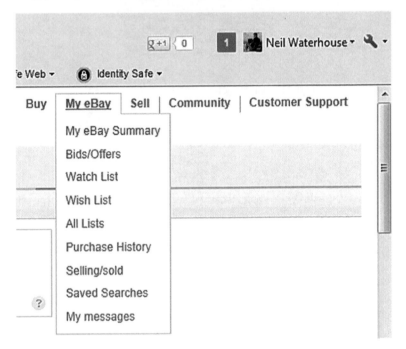

From "My eBay" you get the following options:

My eBay Summary

- The availability of items that you are watching.
- Previous watched items that have sold.
- All purchased items.
- Purchases awaiting your payment.
- Purchases posted.
- Purchases awaiting feedback.

Bids/Offers

- Any bids you have placed.
- Winning bids.
- Losing bids.
- Any offers you have received.
- Active "Best Offers."
- Declined "Best Offers."
- Expired "Best Offers."
- "Second Chance" offers.

Watch List

- Items you are watching that are still available.
- Previous watched items that have sold.

Purchase History

- All purchased items.
- Purchases awaiting your payment.
- Purchases posted.
- Purchases awaiting feedback.

Selling History

- Total sales for the month.
- Total number of items listed.
- Your "Selling Limit." (New eBay accounts have maximum selling limits based on previous sales, i.e., the max may be $2,000 for the month, or it may be 10 items. As eBay gets to know your history, your limits will increase automatically).
- Any items you have scheduled to list.
- Total items listed.
- Items with bids and reserve prices met. (This is a good one to monitor if you list auctions with a BIN price, too).
- Items that are "Available to Sell."
- Pending "Best Offers."

Making Changes to Your Listing

Invariably, you will hit the "submit" button to list your item, then take a gulp and wish you had added something else. No problem! Just go to "My eBay" – "Selling" – click the checkbox next to the listing, and then click the "edit" button.

Note: Auctions which have bids cannot be revised; however eBay *will* allow you to *add text* to the bottom of the listing.

Ending Listings Early

Occasionally, you might list something, only to discover there is something really wrong with your listing or you find out that the item is damaged. You may decide that the best thing to do is simply shut down the listing.

To end a listing, go to "Site Map," which is located at the bottom of every page in eBay. Then, in the middle column, select "End your Listing."

Note: Auctions due to finish in less than 12 hours cannot be ended.

Also note: eBay keeps track of how many times a seller ends listings, so do not end listings unless it is critical to do so. Repeated use can cause your eBay account to be suspended. If you do end a listing early, you will very often receive emails from upset potential buyers who were watching your item.

CHAPTER SEVEN

Handling Questions

"Everyone hears only what he understands."

~ JOHANN WOLFGANG VON GOETHE ~

On eBay, the average ratio of questions to product listings is two: That is two questions per item per day, but you can drop that number of questions substantially.

If you do not want to be bombarded with email questions, try to proactively answer every single question on your ad via text and/ or photos.

Questions are one of the reasons I encourage people to start selling secondhand items they have lying around the house. It is a fast introduction to the sort of questions people ask. In the past, when we used to do a lot of auctions starting at 99 cents, we would always find the quality of the questions would increase with the price. In other words, the cheaper the price, the more ridiculous the questions were; as the price of the auction rose, the more intelligent the questions became.

You learn very quickly to answer every question about postage in your ad; otherwise, you will wake up in the morning to 100 questions asking how much shipping costs to XYZ country. eBay's built-in shipping calculator has already answered a lot of these questions, so please use it.

If you end up sending the same answers to the same questions over and over again, you have four options. You can:

1. Include the question and your response at the bottom of your listing. A checkbox for this option comes with every question sent through eBay messages.

Improve your ad copy, and answer the questions there.

2. Add the answers into the FAQ section of your eBay account (more on this to come).

3. Use email software to record your email replies so that you do not have to keep re-writing the same answers over and over again.

Note: Never joke with customers who you do not know really well. Time and time again, I have seen jokes go over like lead balloons. What can appear amusing to a seller regularly gets taken out of context. Always keep communications professional.

How to Respond to Questions

You can either reply to buyers' questions within eBay through "Messages," or you can reply to eBay emails using programs such as Microsoft Outlook, Gmail, Yahoo, etc.

Both options have pros and cons.

The advantage of replying through eBay messages is that there is a complete history of every email reply, so that eBay representatives can view them if required.

The downside of eBay messages is its limited functionality - like its lack of "canned responses."

Canned Responses

There is a brilliant feature in Google's Gmail called "canned responses," where you can save your email replies and reuse them over and over again with different customers. Gmail is free, and also has the world's best SPAM blocking. Other software you might consider is VisNetic MailFlow.

Canned responses are also great for your feedback. Before we started using canned responses, our morning replies to emails were very long and detailed, but as it approached 5 p.m. on a Friday afternoon, the emails became shorter and shorter. Canned responses keep the quality of the replies up, and massively speeds up the time it takes to answer questions.

If you wish to set up a professional ticked email response system, check out www.hostedsupport.com and / or www.replymanager.com. Remember, to proactively reduce emails, it is important to set up your FAQ page and Smart FAQ.

Smart FAQ's

Smart FAQ's is a free eBay feature that draws on live information from your listings to answer the Top 20 buyer questions *before* buyers reach you through the "Ask a Question" or "Contact Seller" links.

PowerSellers and sellers who are already using FAQ's will automatically have Smart FAQ turned on. Other sellers can turn on

Smart FAQ's by going to My eBay > Site Preferences > Selling Preferences > Manage Communications with Buyers.

You can set up your Smart FAQ's in one of three ways:

1. Direct all buyers to the "Ask a Question" email form if you prefer to answer all of your buyers' questions via email. This option is recommended for small sellers who receive fewer questions.

2. Direct all buyers to the Smart FAQ page where they can look for an answer first before clicking "Contact Seller" to email you directly. This option is recommended for most sellers, especially those who are not always able to answer questions quickly, and those who get a large number of questions.

3. You can change your FAQ's by going to My eBay > My Account > Seller Preferences > FAQ. The FAQ Preference Page allows you to turn FAQ's on and off for all items, make modifications to FAQ's, turn eBay Smart FAQ's on or off, or add your own FAQ's.

CHAPTER EIGHT

Feedback, DSR's and Top-Seller Rating

*"We have two ears and one mouth so that
we can listen twice as much as we speak."*

~ EPICTETUS ~

One week after the purchase of any item on eBay, buyers and sellers are able - and encouraged - to leave feedback for one another.

The feedback options are "Positive," "Neutral," or "Negative," however, **ONLY** buyers can leave negative feedback.

Positive = +1
Neutral = 0
Negative = -1

Each feedback rating that you receive is added to your existing total feedback score (e.g., 1676 feedbacks, as in the picture below):

Top-rated seller

 (1676 ⭐)

99.3% Positive feedback

✔ **Consistently receives highest buyers' ratings**

✔ **Posts items quickly**

✔ **Has earned a track record of excellent service**

The feedback score in the screenshot above is 99.3%, and is calculated based on the number of positive and negative feedbacks in the previous 12 months. The formula for feedbacks is as follows:

$$\frac{positive}{positive + negatives}$$

The star next to the total number of feedbacks contains different colors, representing the amount of feedback ratings the seller has received:

# of Feedbacks	Color of Star
10 to 49	Yellow
50 to 99	Blue
100 to 499	Turquoise
500 to 999	Purple
1000 to 4999	Red
5000 to 9999	Green
10,000 to 24,999	Yellow (shooting star)
25,000 to 49,999	Turquoise (shooting star)
50,000 to 99,999	Purple (shooting star)

100,000 to 499,999	Red (shooting star)
500,000 to 999,999	Green (shooting star)
1,000,000 or more	Silver (shooting star)

Note: If one customer purchases, say, ten items at once, and leaves ten feedbacks (which are either positive or negative), only one of the feedbacks will affect your feedback percentage score.

This is a good thing, as one customer does not have the power to purchase, say, 20 baseball cards for $1 each, and then slam you with 20 negative feedbacks.

Feedback is always scary for new eBayers, but you quickly learn that if you do the right thing, over 99% of buyers will leave you positive feedback. You can use the procedures below to get to 100% if you wish, however maintaining a 100% feedback score is a heavy burden to carry on your back, as you are at the mercy of others who want to give you a hard time just because they are in a bad mood that day.

If your happiness is dependent on maintaining a 100% positive feedback score and, God forbid, someone pushed your feedback score from 100% to 99.9%, then you will not be a happy camper!

Most people want to, and will automatically, leave positive feedback, as long as your item does what it says it will do in your listing, and it arrives in a timely manner - in fact, eBay buyers and sellers have left over seven billion feedbacks for each other since eBay started.

The automatic proviso here is that the customer is able to figure out how to use the product. If a customer requires customer service to get an item working, then you should improve the instructions for that item so that no customer service is required. This will ensure that your positive feedback will be automatic.

By including better instructions for complicated items, you will reduce customer service. By reducing customer service, there is one less thing which can go wrong with the transaction, which, again, improves the feedback you receive.

The other option, which we prefer, is to simply not sell complicated items in the first place! Our rule is, if a ten-year-old cannot figure out how to use it, we don't list it on our eBay stores.

The old saying, "The straw that broke the camel's back," is so true when it comes to eBay feedback. If customers leave negative feedback, it is normally due to the straw that broke the camel's back. That is, the item might have arrived late for some unknown reason, and that was okay, but when they opened the box, they noticed there was not much packing material used, or that the item was packed poorly, so now the item is a bit beaten up, but it appears okay. HOWEVER, the next thing they discover about the item is that, on the listing, it was supposed to come with four batteries and there are only three!

All this (plus it's a full moon, or their dog just ate their favorite slippers) could be enough to push the customer over the edge, leaving you negative feedback. If there had been just one less thing to annoy the customer about this transaction, they may have accepted it without leaving negative feedback. It is rare that a customer will leave negative feedback for one specific problem: usually, it is from a string of things that went wrong.

If an item has a flaw, make sure you document it in your listing. If you don't, the customer will expect it to be flawless when it arrives, and will be disappointed as soon as they lay eyes on it. This just begs for negative feedback. It is better to set up lower expectations for when the item arrives by pointing out the tiniest flaws.

Feedback and DSR's (Detailed Seller Ratings) are extremely important on eBay. Positive feedback and high DSR's are easy to accumulate if you do the right thing. Sure, some buyers may leave some negatives - all large sellers receive some - but that, to a certain extent, is "just the cost of doing business" through eBay, and compared to the benefits, is very insignificant.

The secret is to know how to minimize the amount of negative feedbacks, and low DSR's, that you receive so you can keep your feedback score close to 100%, and keep your DSR's high enough to achieve and maintain Top Rated seller status.

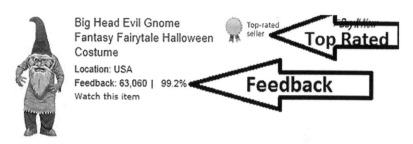

The secret to getting a good night's sleep when owning an eBay business is to NOT become emotionally attached to what a customer writes, in the event that you receive negative feedback. Instead, ask yourself if you can improve something in your business. Always look at the big picture. The big picture is your entire eBay business, not just this one transaction for which you received a negative feedback. Yes, some people can be nasty: perhaps they just had an argument with their spouse! If you jump on the phone, they will usually, immediately, change their tune, and be nice as pie. They normally just want to feel understood.

Let me repeat that, they normally just want to feel understood.

Always listen, and let them know you understand how they feel.

Again, always listen, and let them know you understand how they feel.

More often that not, you can get the buyer to revise their negative feedback.

To do this:

1. Sign in to your eBay account.
2. Click on "Site Map" at the bottom of the page.

3. Under the "Community" tab, click on "Request Feedback Revision."

4. Choose which customer you want to send the feedback revision link to.

Sometimes, you will have to accept something back, and refund maybe $50 for an item that was obviously damaged by the customer. When this happens, you might immediately think, "I'm not going to let that person walk all over me!" however the smart thing is to think about the big picture of your whole eBay business: Is it worth receiving a negative feedback for a 50 dollar sale?

When damaged stock (or stock that is flawed and cannot be re-sold as new) is returned to you, you can very often sell the damaged item on eBay using the auction format. We have always been blown away by how high a price damaged items sell for. (Buyers seem to think they are getting a bargain when they buy a damaged item). We have always joked about how we should sell all of our stock as "Damaged!"

Try to stay emotionally disconnected. Quickly grow your business so you can have someone else answer your emails for you. This makes it much easier to stay emotionally detached when to comes to customer complaints. Make sure you pay the staff member a bonus for keeping your feedback above a certain percentage. If your feedback is, say, 99.5% when your customer service representative starts working, offer them a monthly bonus if they get your feedback score to 99.6%, and a higher monthly bonus for higher feedback ratings.

I received my first negative feedback very shortly after I started on eBay. I had a bucket of old sockets in the garage, manufactured by a quality company called Sidchrome.

I listed these on eBay as "Assorted Sidchrome sockets." They sold, and I mailed them to the buyer, not thinking any further about them. It wasn't until many weeks later that I noticed my feedback rating had dropped from 100% to less than 90%. (I only had five feedbacks, so one negative feedback made a big difference)!

Yikes! What had happened? I clicked on my feedback and saw that the buyer who purchased the sockets had written, "Not all sockets were Sidchrome."

In hindsight, I realized I hadn't understood the importance of feedback, and consequently never double-checked all the sockets before listing them. Oops! Lesson learned!

Of course, the customer could have contacted me to ask for some sort of compensation, however I was the one who made the mistake of not double-checking before listing, and therefore I had no one to blame but myself.

We stopped using that eBay account due to the low feedback, but after 12 months the negative feedback finally disappeared, and our rating on that account was, once again, restored to 100%.

eBay feedback is a tough subject. I have been to many eBay seminars (which eBay has either hosted or is attending) and people have continually stood up to whinge and moan about the negative feedback they have received. I have to admit, I have been very tempted to as well. HOWEVER, feedback is what made eBay successful: It is why the public trusts eBay sellers to send their products when buyers hand over their money. You have to either learn to work with the eBay feedback system, or find another business.

Running an eBay business is different from running other businesses. Customers act as if they are your only customer. Customers will send emails like, "Have you sent my item yet?" without their names or details. Sometimes, when a customer returns an item, they will mail it back with neither name nor invoice, expecting you to know who they are.

We have two sets of rules: One for eBay sales which have been purchased within the last 60 days and are pending feedback (eBay buyers can leave feedback for 60 days from the date of purchase); and a different, more conventional set of business rules for eBay customers who *have* left feedback, or have purchased from our non-eBay website.

For every eBay business we have, we also have a website selling the same products, and the rules are different for both businesses.

With an eBay business, the answer is "Yes" when a customer asks for something (sometimes followed by blocking them from ever purchasing from us again through eBay). With our web stores, the answer is "Why?" (The same as other businesses).

Don't get me wrong: Customer service is not a bad thing - it is just the cost of doing business on eBay. The huge traffic to your listings, and the profit rewards on eBay, far outweigh the extra attention that eBay customers can require.

Sure, there are some real @#$holes out there with chips on their shoulders who are just looking for some way to vent their anger, and the feedback button looks as good a place as any! We have even had people write "Great product" on their feedback, and then click on the negative feedback button! However, most people will leave positive feedback if you do the right thing.

Tips for Maintaining High Feedback

1. Don't exaggerate, in any way, on your listing. Only write what is 100% true and correct.
2. If you are selling any used items that have marks and scratches, make sure to include these in the ad, via text and/or photos.
3. Fast shipment: Try to always ship within one business day of receiving payment.
4. Pack the item really well. If you believe that most freight companies have a quick round of football with the packages you send out, then you would not be far off. Don't be fooled into thinking that by putting a "Fragile" sticker on a box, that the employees at the local post/freight depot will take better care of it: I guarantee you, they won't! I think a "Fragile" sticker translates into, "Let's drop this box to see if we can hear the contents break!" When we import items, we are always asking ourselves, "Will this item withstand a fall from the back of a truck (approx 3-4 feet) onto the road

packed in reasonable condition?" If the answer is "no", we do not import it.

5. Emails. Make sure all emails are answered within one business day. If a customer is having a hard time with a product, pick up the phone and give them a quick call. It is amazing how a quick phone call can diffuse situations. If the customer is heated, MAKE SURE you shut up and listen. MAKE SURE the customer realizes that you DO understand their frustration. If the customer is overseas, you can call overseas for cheap these days, using either long distance phone cards (which are available from places like news stands), or do what we do, and use Skype to call. With Skype, you can purchase credit to call any country for the same price as a local call. The cost of calling a mobile phone number in other countries becomes similar to calling a mobile number in your own country. For more information, go to http://www.skype.com

6. If an item is faulty, replace it. Remember, you can resell damaged stock, and faulty items *should* be replaced by the manufacturer.

7. Don't set up unreal expectations. Be careful with lines like, "Same Day Shipping," or "24 Hour Shipping," as many customers think their purchase will arrive in one day, even if you are in Hawaii and the customer is in Russia! Sure, lines like this improve sales, but the low feedback, low DSR's, and the loss of your Top Rated seller status will come around and bite you on the backside.

8. Postage prices. Make sure your postage prices are crystal clear in your ad copy, and never charge more than you advertise. Even better, do not post any postage prices in your ad. Instead, use eBay's free postage calculator. To use eBay's shipping calculator, just enter the dimensions and the weight of the item when listing, and select how you are going to ship the item (i.e., via UPS). By doing this, every customer, no matter where they are on the planet, will

see the postage price to their front door. These quotes are dependable because they are accurate: eBay knows exactly where you live, and where the buyer lives. The shipping information is then pulled from pre-loaded rate sheets. The good thing about this is, if you have a better rate (with, say, UPS) than eBay quotes on the rate sheets they use, you can make money on shipping. If you post an item with a stamp, and the stamp reads $5, then do not charge any more for postage than $5! Yep, I can hear all the business people screaming, "What about the envelope, the box, my time to pack it up, and the drive to the post office!?" Yep, I MORE than understand. HOWEVER: many buyers don't understand, or have not thought this through, and *they are the ones with their fingers hovering over the feedback button*. All is not lost! The solution is to stop using stamps, as quickly as possible. Stamps are like big red flags to buyers, telling the customer exactly how much it cost to mail the item. Couriers like Fedex, DHL, etc., do not mark in the parcel how much you paid. In Australia, we use Eparcel, who also do not reveal how much we pay. In the U.S., you can also use www.stamps.com which does not display postage charges. Look at other eBay listings to study how successful eBay sellers ship in your country.

9. If you get a customer who is unreasonable, or just a huge pain in the proverbial @#$, you can block them from buying from you again. To do this, go to: http://pages.eBay.com/help/sell/manage_bidders_ov.html

10. Give refunds when necessary. All businesses have to give refunds from time to time. Always remember: Think of the big picture, which is your entire eBay business/feedback score (even if you know the customer is wrong, or is an arrogant &#%?@! - just refund them and wish them well). Your goal is to win by way of your massive success from

building your eBay empire; not to win arguments with a few arrogant customers.

Note: Only sellers can receive negative feedback. Also note: Buyers can only leave feedback for 60 days from the purchase date.

To see the feedback on your eBay account, or of other sellers', just click on any of your/their products, and then click on the feedback button, which is located on the right-hand side of the page:

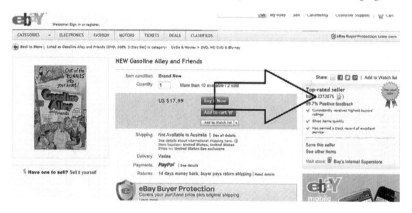

If you look at the feedback ratings for successful sellers, almost all of them are getting some negative feedback every month. If you set your goal in life to always have 100% positive feedback, then you had better also sign up for some blood pressure medication, as you are putting a lot of pressure on yourself. You do need high feedback, however, maintaining a 100% feedback score is not critical for a million or multi-million dollar eBay business.

It *is* critical, though, to use steps and procedures to maintain a feedback rating of greater than 98%, and to maintain Top Rated seller status. That way you can sleep at night, knowing that you have enough control over your procedures to avoid freaking out if some customer has a bad hair day and wishes to take it out on you (via eBay's feedback system).

By clicking on any eBay member's feedback score, it will take you to a history of their eBay transactions, as pictured in the screenshot below:

From here, you can also see the following:

- The seller's ID (and if they have changed their ID in the last 30 days).
- Any feedback written for this seller, from other buyers and sellers.
- Detailed sellers ratings.
- Feedback left by this seller.
- Which items the seller has sold, and for what price, in the last 90 days.

If you click on any of the feedback numbers (pictured above), you can see the exact feedback left.

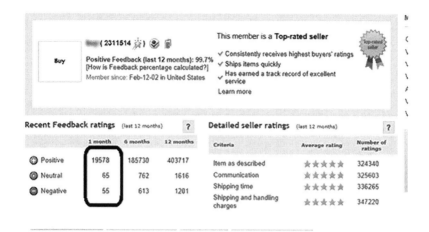

Below: The positive feedback, after I clicked on "19578" from the screenshot above.

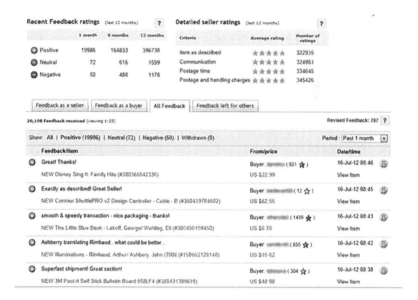

If you look at the feedback of large sellers, almost all of them are getting some negative feedback every month:

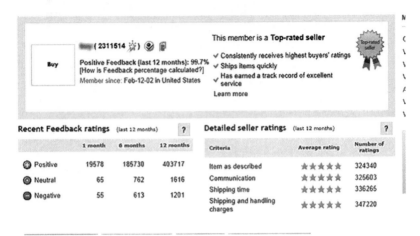

When you do get NF (negative feedback), it's not the end of the world. Very often, you can call the customer to resolve the issue. You can then send them the "Remove Negative Feedback" link. We do this all the time.

Besides negotiating with the customers to change their negative feedback, and then sending them the link so that they can change it, you can also ask eBay to remove negative feedback in the following instances:

- When feedback is in violation of eBay's "Feedback Abuse" policy. For instance:
  - ➤ If a buyer includes a seller's username or phone number in a feedback comment, eBay will remove the feedback upon request of the seller.
  - ➤ If a seller blocks a buyer from bidding on his items using the eBay Blocked Bidder feature, and a buyer creates another user ID to get around the block, wins the item, and then leaves negative feedback, eBay will remove the feedback upon request of the seller.

- If negative feedback was intended for another user it will be considered for removal, only when the user responsible for the negative feedback informs eBay that it was mistakenly placed into the seller's account. The feedback will then be posted to the correct user.
- If feedback was left by someone who is ineligible to participate in eBay transactions, according to Section 1 of the eBay User Agreement (e.g., suspended users, users that are no longer members, users that are flagged for violations determined by eBay, etc.), at the time of the transaction or at the time the feedback was left.
- If feedback has nothing to do with the transaction in question.
- If a user provides eBay with false contact information, and cannot be contacted.
- If left by a buyer who set up their eBay account using fraudulent information.
- If a user bids on or purchases an item, with no intention of completing the transaction, solely to gain the opportunity to leave negative feedback for the seller.
- If the person who left the feedback can be identified as a minor.
- If left by users who are indefinitely suspended for certain policy violations. eBay takes the position that members who are indefinitely suspended shouldn't be able to permanently impact another member's account.
- If feedback contains a URL link or Java script.
- If eBay receives a court order stating that the feedback is slanderous, defamatory, or otherwise illegal.
- If feedback refers to any investigation, whether by eBay or a law enforcement agency.
- If a buyer fails to respond to the "Unpaid Item" process and/or an "Unpaid Item" strike.
- If feedback contains any personal, identifying information about the seller.

- If feedback is deemed as harassment.
- If the listing meets the Customs Requirements (below), but the seller receives a negative or neutral feedback comment which references customs delays or customs fees.
- If feedback contains vulgar, foul, or profane language.

Note: Make sure you include a Customs Requirement like the following in all of your listings and templates:

International Buyers – Please Note:
Import duties, taxes and charges are not included in the item price or postage charges. These charges are the buyer's responsibility. Please check with your country's customs office to determine what these additional costs will be, prior to bidding/buying.

Responding to Negative Feedback

If someone leaves you negative feedback, you are able to defend yourself (sort of) by posting your defense under their negative feedback. The reason I say "sort of" is that if you do write anything in your defense, the customer is allowed the LAST and final chance to respond. If the customer is already mad, and you defend yourself, guess what they are going to write!

Be very careful with this. Only write a defense if you are 100% positive the customer is now happy.

To respond to feedback, click the feedback link in the drop-down menu in the account tab on the "My eBay" page, and then click the "Go to Feedback Forum" link at the top of the page.

eBay can also remove feedback due to "feedback extortion," described as follows:

- Threatening to leave negative or neutral feedback for another member (unless the other member provides goods or services not included in the original listing) is not permitted.

- Buyers are not allowed to threaten sellers with negative feedback, neutral feedback, or low Detailed Seller Ratings in order to obtain goods or services not included in the original listing.

DSR's

Possibly even more important than feedback ratings is the DSR (Detailed Seller Rating).

You can view other sellers' DSR's by clicking on their feedback:

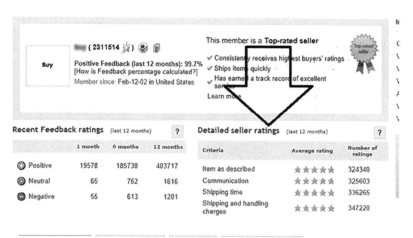

The best way for you to see your own DSR is through the eBay dashboard.

To get there; click on "My eBay" – "Account" – "Seller dashboard."

Seller dashboard

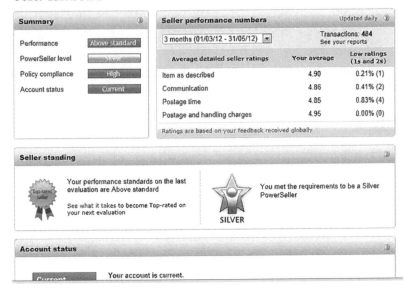

The DSR's are four different ratings (on a 1-5 scale) which eBay requests buyers to leave after they purchase an item from eBay. The four areas for the ratings are:

- Item as Described
- Communication
- Shipping Time
- Shipping and Handling Charges

If a seller receives enough low DSR's to qualify as below "industry standard," then the seller will be penalized. (The "industry standard" is the average of other sellers). If one of your DSR's drops below 4.6, your listings may not show at all.

The account below is from one of my students who has a 100% feedback score, but they lost their Top Rated seller status due to low DSR's. (More on the Top Rated seller status later).

Seller dashboard

I was able to show the seller how to fix the problem with the low DSR's: by removing the phrase "Same Day Shipping." The seller was then able to set more realistic expectations for buyers.

DSR scores are calculated over a three-month period and evaluated by eBay on a monthly basis.

If your DSR's are lower than 4.9, simply compare what other, similar sellers are doing differently. Purchase something cheap from them, and monitor the following processes: What kind of emails do they send you? Which shipping method do they use? Are you promising more than they are, but delivering less?

Note: Postage issues are almost always the cause of a low DSR. This is another reason to evaluate free shipping.

Top-Seller Rating

Top-rated seller

 (15053 ⭐) me

99.5% Positive feedback

✔ Consistently receives highest buyers' ratings

✔ Posts items quickly

✔ Has earned a track record of excellent service

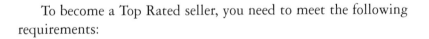

Save this seller

See other items

Visit store:

To become a Top Rated seller, you need to meet the following requirements:

- Consistently earn 4- or 5-star ratings from eBay buyers.
- Sell $3,000 or more every year.
- Sell a minimum of 100 items on eBay every year.

If you meet the above requirements, and have good enough DSR's, you will automatically receive the Top Rated seller logo on all your listings. If you are ranked by eBay as a Top Rated seller, your listings will be shown 33% more.

Here is the bottom line for maintaining high feedback: *Under-promise and over-deliver, and if you do receive a negative feedback, immediately jump on the phone to the customer.*

When to Leave Feedback

There are two thoughts on this: Do you leave feedback for your buyers before, or after, they leave feedback for you?

The first thought, and perhaps the fairest option, is to leave positive feedback as soon as a buyer pays, as many would agree that the buyer has done everything that has been asked of them (i.e., paid for their products).

The second strategy is to leave feedback after they have left you positive feedback. The thought behind this is that if the customer is not happy, they may not leave you negative feedback, fearing that you will also leave negative feedback for them.

In the past, this could be done, but sellers are no longer able to leave negative feedback for buyers. (Most buyers, however, do not know this).

We have tested both options, and it is so close that it is very difficult to choose which strategy works the best. We have chosen to always leave feedback first.

CHAPTER NINE

Adding an eBay Store

"It only takes a match to light an inferno"

~ Author unknown ~

What is an eBay Store?

Once you have built up to 25 transactions-plus a week, an eBay store will almost certainly be more economical for you, as the fees are lower for eBay store owners. You can also list items for longer durations, which cut down on the workload of continually re-listing items. Once you get bigger, you can automate this process using third-party software. (More on this later).

Being an eBay store owner, you also get access to subscription tools to manage listings, selling, doing feedback in volume, along with tools for market research, accounting, and store "web traffic" analysis.

You also get an online "storefront" integrated into eBay's own site, to which you can send customers and repeat buyers.

There are additional tools and features that eBay provides once you own an eBay store - far too many to list here.

To check out all of the available features of an eBay store, go to: http://pages.eBay.com/storefronts/start.html

Because of the lower fees and tools, high-volume sellers and sellers of low-demand, high-value items often find that owning eBay stores provides a better, more economical, lower-overhead way to leverage eBay's huge, international customer base.

Requirements

To own an eBay store, you must meet one of the following criteria:

- Have a feedback profile of 20 or higher
- Be "ID Verified"
- Have a PayPal account in good standing

There is a monthly subscription fee, depending on the size of the store you want to maintain. At the time of press, subscriptions started at $15.95 USD per month for a basic store, which manages up to 250 listings per day. However, eBay regularly changes fees, and most countries charge different fees. Later in this chapter, I will show you how to find out the fees for your country.

Think of the store fees as shop rent, but unlike paying rent for a conventional shop, your shop is located in the busiest marketplace on the planet: eBay.

Once you are able to meet one of the above requirements, opening an eBay store is as easy as visiting the "Open an eBay Store" link.

Why Open an eBay Store?

All sellers who have an eBay store will have the little red door displayed (as in the screenshot above). An eBay store gives you a number of marketing tools that you can use to promote your store, such as email marketing, a customized listing header, promotional flyers, cross-promotions, RSS feeds, and the ability to link your external store (if you own one), as long as it can be found through Google. You can also add the URL of your store onto any marketing material you might have.

The other huge reason to consider opening an eBay store is for lower listing fees. eBay fees continually change, and are different in most countries, so it is best to check your country's eBay site for your country's eBay fees. To find fees for your country, log into eBay, then click on "Site Map," which is located at the bottom of the page:

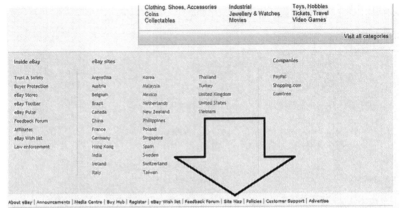

Then click on the "A-Z Index" in "Help Topics":

Then select "F" for fees:

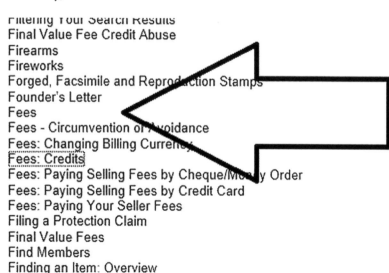

A-Z Index of Help Topics

A B C D E F G H I J K L M N O P Q R S
T U V W-Z All

About Me Page
About eBay Picture Services
About Me
About Me Guidelines (Policy)
About Me HTML Tags
About Me Pages
About Postage Services
Abuse of the Feedback System
Abuse of Final Value Fee Credit
Academic Software (Policy)
Account: Closing Your eBay Account
Account: Creating for Selling
Account Guard: detecting spoof Web sites
Account Status: Viewing Selling Activity
Account Takeover: Securing Your Account

Lastly, select "Fees":

Filtering Your Search Results
Final Value Fee Credit Abuse
Firearms
Fireworks
Forged, Facsimile and Reproduction Stamps
Founder's Letter
Fees
Fees - Circumvention of Avoidance
Fees: Changing Billing Currency
Fees: Credits
Fees: Paying Selling Fees by Cheque/Money Order
Fees: Paying Selling Fees by Credit Card
Fees: Paying Your Seller Fees
Filing a Protection Claim
Final Value Fees
Find Members
Finding an Item: Overview

In Australia (at this time of writing), the fees for casual sellers (vs. PowerSellers and/or sellers who are registered business owners) are as follows:

eBay Fees

Listing Fees

First 30 listings	Free
31 + items	Sales price dependent
Less than $20	50 cents
$20 - $99	$1.50
$100 or more	$3.00

Final Value Fees

First 30 listings	7.9% (capped at $100)
31+ items	7.9% (uncapped)

"Listing fees" are charged when you list an item.

"Final Value fees" are charged only when your item has sold.

For example, let's say you list a used sewing machine for auction, and decide to start the auction at 99 cents. This is the 31st item you have listed this month, so you have used up your 30 free credits. The listing fee will be 50 cents.

The sewing machine winds up selling for $100, thus incurring a FVF (Final Value Fee) of $7.90 ($100 x 7.9% = $7.90).

Thus, your total fees are $8.40. (The 50 cent Listing fee plus the $7.90 Final Value fee, which equals $8.40).

Cars, boats and aircraft have different fee structures, which are not the topic of this book. For these fees, check on the eBay site in your country.

Now, let's look at the fees if you open an eBay store.

Store Fees

Store Type

Basic and Featured Stores	$24.95 per month
Anchor Stores	$499.95 per month

Insertion Fee for BIN

Basic and Featured Stores	20 cents
Anchor Stores	Free

Insertion Fee for Auction

Listing Start Price	Insertion Fee
Less than $20	50 cents
$20 - $99	$1.50
$100 or more	$3.00

Final Value Fees for Auction and BIN

Basic and Featured Store	7% of the closing price, excluding postage (capped at $100).
Anchor Store	6% of the closing price, excluding postage (capped at $100).

eBay Store Versus No eBay Store

Once you have consistently sold more than the equivalent of $2,000 USD per month for three consecutive months, you will automatically become a PowerSeller. As a PowerSeller, you no longer qualify for 30 free listings. Let's look at the fees for a seller who does not have an eBay store and sells 100 items per month, at an average price of $75:

Listing Fees	Total Listing Fees for 100 items	Final Value Fees @7.5%	Total Final Value Fees for 100 items @ $75 EACH
50 cents per listing	$50	$75 x 7.5% x 100	$563
Total Fees $613			

Now let's have a look at the fees if you do have an eBay store.

Listing Fees	Total Listing Fees for 100 items	Final Value Fees @ 7%	Total Final Value Fees for 100 items @ $75 EACH
20 cents per listing	$20	$75 x 7.% x 100	$525
Total Fees $570			

This is a $43 savings, plus you get all the store's other features, too. Of course, the more you sell, the more you save with an eBay store. When you grow large enough, an Anchor Store will save you even more money.

A quick way of calculating fees is to use Ryan Olbe's free eBay fee calculator, at http://www.rolbe.com/eBay.htm

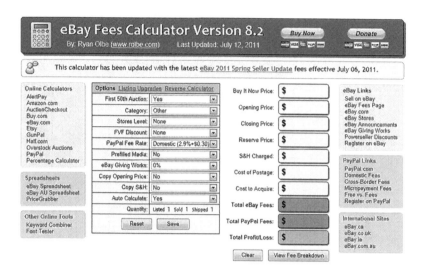

You can also download spreadsheets to do this, but Ryan charges a small fee for those.

Store Design

You can create a good-looking store by using eBay's built-in store templates, or you can have an even fancier one created by a web design company like Volusion (www.volusion.com), Frooition (www.frooition.com), or OCdesigns (www.ocdesigns.com). To find other eBay store designers, Google "eBay store design." Make sure you get at least three quotes, and ask to see their portfolio. Creating an eBay storefront is different than creating a website: Make sure you choose a designer who has experience working with eBay storefronts.

To view examples of other sellers' stores, just click on the red door in any listings where the seller has a store.

When you are starting out, don't go overboard creating a fancy-looking store - just keep it clean and simple. Buyers love clean, simple sites without fancy, flashing icons, or fireworks going off in the corner, or little things scrolling across the screen: Yuck, yuck, yuck!

Buyers and computer users like clean and simple. Look at Google, for instance. Most of the screen is white, with a search box in the middle!

Only a small percentage of eBay buyers visit stores, and even less purchase from them. Most buyers either use the search box in eBay to search for an item to buy, or scroll through the different categories.

CHAPTER TEN

Opening a Website with the Same Products

*"Now that it's all over, what did you really do
yesterday that's worth mentioning?"*

~COLEMAN COX ~

A great way to double your eBay sales (and more) is to open a website
that sells exactly the same products as you sell on eBay. You can
then send traffic to your website from places like Google Adwords.
Through Google Adwords, you can buy clicks to your website.
That is, every time you run an ad for your website on Google, and
somebody clicks the ad you display (taking them to your website),
Google charges you. This is called "PPC advertising," or "Pay Per
Click" advertising.

The secret of PPC advertising is to get your ad campaigns running profitably so that they have an ROI (Return on Investment) of
greater than one. For instance, if you spend $1 on advertising, you
need to make back more than a $1 profit. If you make a $2 profit

for every $1 you spend, we call this an ROI of two (i.e., every $1 spent creates $2 profit).

So often, I am asked, "How much should I spend on PPC advertising?" My answer is always the same: "If you have not proven the ROI, spend no more than $20 at a time to test."

If you *have* proven the ROI to be greater than one over a three-month period or more, then I always say, "Best to spend 1 million dollars." Then I watch their mouths drop!

BUT, why wouldn't you? If you had proven, over time, that every time you spent $1 on PPC advertising, you got back $2, why wouldn't you spend one million or more?

The screenshot above is from one of our Google Adwords campaigns, where we have spent over one million dollars. You can see where we test the ads and then open the throttle to get as many clicks as possible.

Many people I speak to think of advertising as a cost.

It is only a cost if it has an ROI of less than one.

If it has an ROI of greater than one, then it is a license to print money.

I am not going to go into the how-to of PPC advertising here, as that is a whole new subject. If you are interested in PPC advertising, I would HIGHLY recommend you do not spend one cent until you read Perry Marshall's *Definitive Guide To Adwords* http://www.

perry-marshall.org Perry is the go-to guy I use whenever I have a question about Google advertising.

If you decide to open your own website, the first thing you need to do is purchase a domain name (e.g., "xyz.com").

To find sellers of domain names, Google "domain names." (I purchase mine from Ghost Name, at http://www.ghostname.com). There are thousands of domain name hosting companies out there, but make sure the one you choose has 24/7 telephone support, high bandwidth (speed), and most importantly, high reliability. If you are buying traffic for your website, you cannot afford to have your site down for one minute. Not only does this cost money in lost sales, but Google can "black flag" your site. Google does not want its users to end up at a faulty or down website.

Domain names vary in price, from less than $15 up to "the sky is the limit." Price depends on how many characters it has, and how popular the word/s are (i.e., "www.ibm.com" would be worth a small - or probably more like a large – fortune, as it only has three characters (but, of course, the company IBM owns them). At the time of writing, www.eye-bee-emm.com, is available for $12.95. It sounds similar, but it has 11 characters. (Of course, I am not suggesting you buy it, I am just using this as an example).

Once you have purchased a domain name, the next step is to have the name "hosted." That is, you pay a company like Ghost Name (or any other hosting company) to store your website on one of their servers (preferably a fast one), so that when a customer clicks on something in your store (like a picture), it loads quickly on their computer. This is where a good hosting company becomes critical, especially if you are doing PPC advertising, because Google penalizes websites with slow servers.

Google's number one goal is to give its users the best experience possible. Google does not specialize in taking searchers to slow-loading websites.

For your website, unless you have HTML experience with an HTML editing program (such as Dreamweaver), you will need to get someone to create one for you. Most websites are written using web programming language like HTML or PHP.

There are specialized web design companies, such as Frooition (http://www.frooition.com), who are regulars at trade shows. All of the sites they have created for their customers (from what I have seen) looked professionally done.

Branding

Branding is a popular word bandied about the Internet seminars, and I have heard many different explanations as to what it means.

The best interpretation I've heard was given by an eBay employee. He said, "Branding is your 'gut feeling' about a product, service or a business."

Pause, and think about that for a moment before reading on.

Take the Nike organization for instance: Most people's gut feeling is that they make *high quality* shoes.

Let's say you walk into a store and you see some Nike shoes that are selling for $200, and next to them is an almost identical pair made by a Chinese company that you have never heard of, which are also selling for $200. Which ones do you purchase?

Obviously, the Nike pair will outsell the generic brand every time. Why? Because most people perceive Nike as being high quality due to the Nike branding. Because of this perceived quality (branding), Nike can charge a ton more money for their shoes, even if they were to come out of the same factory as the cheaper ones.

We can also easily create branding for our eBay businesses and websites. It is important to do this in the proper order: i.e., create your eBay store first and your website second, so that the website looks very similar to the store. It is essential to keep the look (branding) the same in both, so that when customers are in either, they feel at home.

Take a look at other large eBay stores to view their branding. To find the most successful eBay sellers, go to http://pulse.eBay.com/ and you will see five who have the largest number of listings:

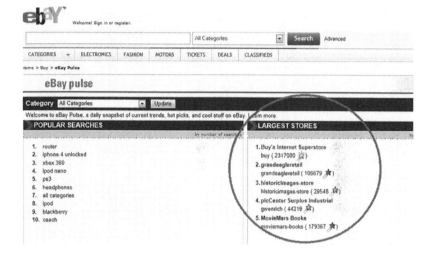

When you are looking through other sellers' sites to get ideas, always ask yourself these questions within the first 10 seconds: What is your gut feeling telling you? Is the site messy, or is it making you feel relaxed? Are the products cheap? Expensive? Do you want to be on this site, looking at this product, reading this ad, or are you dying to hit the back button? What do you like/dislike: is it the colors, the space, the clutter, the pictures, (etc.)?

If you are not a creative person, you can just look at a successful eBay store to see what the sellers have done, and then do something similar. By successful, I mean that the sellers have lots of feedback (e.g., 50,000 plus), with Top Rated seller status and feedback scores of at least 99.5%.

Here is another way to find large eBay sellers.

Search for any product on eBay. In this case, I will search for "gnome."

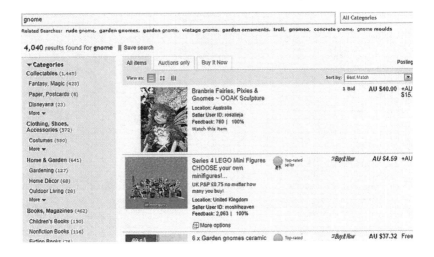

When eBay shows you the search results, click on any item from the results above. I will click on "Branbria Fairies."

Then, click on their feedback (as per the pic, below). In this case, I clicked on "760."

There, you will see feedback scores from all the other eBay buyers and sellers who have had transactions with this seller. If there are no high-scoring ones there, just click on any one of those feedback scores and repeat the process, until you find an eBay seller with feedback greater than 50,000.

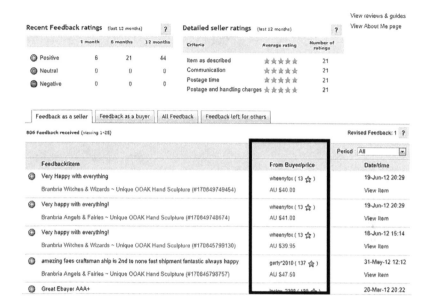

Repeat Sales

Your website is a great place to get repeat sales. With all of our eBay businesses, we attach a discount card promoting our website with every item we post out. It is a great way to let customers know you have a website. The discount card offers 10% off for all future purchases from the website. (This discount card is the same size as a business card).

It is seven times easier to sell to an existing customer than it is to get a brand new one.

Up sells: Would You Like Fries with That?

Up selling (i.e., "Would you like fries with that?") is very profitable. McDonalds serves approximately 47,000,000 customers around the world, daily. If McDonalds up sells 1 in 5 customers, globally, per day, that's 7,833,334 up sells per day. If the up sell is for just $1.00, they make almost 8 million dollars of extra revenue per day. If the up sell is for a simple order of large fries (about $2.00), McDonalds brings in an additional $15,666,668 per day.

With a website, you can use automation software to automatically up sell items. For instance, if a customer purchases a garden gnome, you can up sell them a garden fairy, or garden lights, or anything else which you have in stock that is relevant to their purchase. (More on automation in Chapter 11).

Email List

This is how you can sell goods fast, for no eBay or advertising fees. You can make a lot of money with email blasts, and, at the time of writing, it is still free to email. You can accumulate a list of email addresses by recording the email address of every customer who communicates with you.

Let's say, over time, you accumulate email addresses, and you now have a database of, say, 5,000 email addresses. If you send an email blast to your database, advertising a product in your store which sells for, say, $100 and makes a $50 profit, and only 1% of the email blast recipients purchase it, you have just made $2,500 from writing one email!

We do these email blasts at least once a week.

It does not take long to build up an email list. If you have just 10 products and sell on average 10 per week of each product, that is 100 sales/email addresses in 1 week! Over 12 months you have the potential to collect over 5000 email addresses, and that is with only 10 products.

We use Constant Contact (http://www.constantcontact.com) to manage our email database; however, there are plenty of other email marketing companies. To find a company, Google "email marketing."

When to Email

We have tested all different days and times to determine when to email, and have settled on every Tuesday at 9:30 a.m., and most Thursdays at 9:30 a.m.

Special dates are especially good for email marketing, i.e., Mother's Day Sales, Father's Day Sales, Easter Sales, Spring Sales, End-of-Financial Year Sales, etc., etc.

To get ideas for emails, sign up for email newsletters from other eBay and non-eBay sellers.

Amazon

Another way of doubling your sales without increasing the number of different items you have is to sell the same exact products on Amazon (www.amazon.com) that you sell on eBay.

Many people still think of Amazon as only a site on which to buy books; however, this is far from the case. Amazon has been growing by over 30%, year after year, and not just because of book sales. Today, Amazon sells anything and everything, and is the fastest growing ecommerce website on the planet with last year's sales growing at a staggering 44%! Amazon at the time of press has over 180 million customers and you can easily be one of the sellers to these 180 million customers.

The sellers on Amazon vary, from Ma and Pa selling out of their basement to large corporations.

With Amazon, I always urge my coaching clients to get all the systems and procedures running smoothly on their eBay business and websites before selling on Amazon, as Amazon is even more dependent on feedback than eBay: If you mess around with Amazon customers, Amazon will ban you forever.

CHAPTER ELEVEN

Automation Tools

"Doing business without advertising is like winking at a girl in the dark. You know what you are doing, but nobody else does."

~ STEUART HENDERSON BRITT ~

There is nothing that I love more about an online business than the automation which can be implemented. Many people, when they go into a business of their own, start with a dream of making lots of money and taking lots of time off but, within a year, they are very often working longer hours than they used to when they were working for someone else, and being paid less than they would be paid if they worked for someone else.

You can also fall into that trap with an eBay/online business.

The secret is to get out of doing all of the tasks which you can palm off on either someone else or (preferably) a software program.

Whenever I am given the choice of employing a person or installing a new piece of hardware/software, I will almost always go with the hardware/software, as it is more reliable, and normally tons cheaper. Plus, a computer can't trip over a box and sue you!

Always look at the tasks you are doing to see if it is cheaper to pay someone else to do it for you. That is, if you are doing all the packing but you can pay, say, a part-time mom to do it for you, and the mom costs, say, $10 per hour, this means that you are only worth $10 per hour while you are packing. However, if you pay someone else to do the packing, then you can use that time to do something more productive (like writing a new ad or researching new products) which can make you in excess of $100 per hour.

The same goes with all tasks: If you spend, say, three hours every day cleaning your own house, you are only worth the same amount as you can pay a cleaner to do it for you. If the cleaner costs you, say, $15 per hour, and you can make any more than $15 per hour doing something else, you should not be cleaning your own house - unless you enjoy it!

Use the same costing strategy to work out when it is time to spend money on hardware and software.

Turbo Lister

The first semi-automation tool to learn for a new eBay business is eBay's own "Turbo Lister." Turbo Lister is designed for small to medium size sellers. Turbo Lister is free to download from eBay. Turbo Lister enables you to create listings offline on your computer. Then, when you are ready, you can upload the listing to eBay.

The HUGE difference with Turbo Lister is that it runs from your computer offline, so it does not require the Internet what-soever while you are creating your listing. This means that if you encounter an Internet glitch, you have not lost all of your work!

With Turbo Lister, you do not have to create each listing in one sitting. You can do a bit, save it, come back later, and do some more. Turbo Lister then saves your listings so that you can use them over and over again when relisting identical items. You can also "synchronize/import" any existing listings that you already have on eBay into Turbo Lister, so that you can edit or relist them from your own PC.

The main features of Turbo Lister allow you to:

- Create listings using a built-in design editor and built-in templates (no HTML knowledge needed).
- List multiple items at the same time.
- Duplicate existing listings, and save listings to reuse again and again.
- Change formats, or add item specifics to multiple items, all at once.
- Access HTML templates.
- Upload thousands of listings to eBay with a single click.
- Add photos and preview your listings without being connected to the Internet.
- Insert payment, tax, and shipping terms (and any other messages you want to include) into your listings.
- Import active or completed item listings from eBay to Turbo Lister.
- Edit or revise active listings on eBay.
- Relist and sell similar items on eBay.
- Save listing information for future listings.

How to download Turbo Lister:

- Go to any page in eBay.
- Click the "Site map" button at the very bottom of the page:

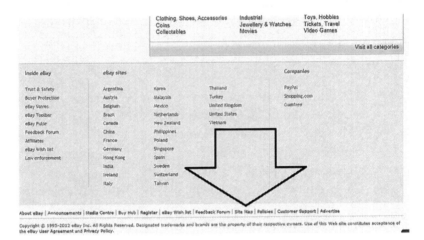

- Under "Selling Tools," click on "Turbo Lister" (as per the pic, below):

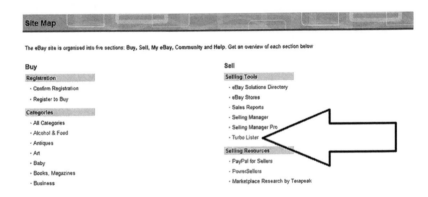

- Then click on "Turbo Lister" (as per the picture below) to begin the download.

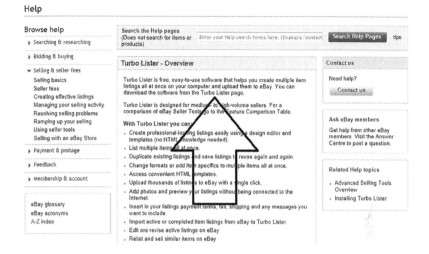

Help

Browse help

▸ Searching & researching

▸ Bidding & buying

▾ Selling & seller fees
  Selling basics
  Seller fees
  Creating effective listings
  Managing your selling activity
  Resolving selling problems
  Ramping up your selling
  Using seller tools
  Selling with an eBay Store

▸ Payment & postage

▸ Feedback

▸ Membership & account

  eBay glossary
  eBay acronyms
  A-Z index

Search the Help pages
(Does not search for items or products)

Enter your Help search terms here. (Example: contact   [Search Help Pages]   tips

Turbo Lister - Overview

Turbo Lister is free, easy-to-use software that helps you create multiple item listings all at once on your computer and upload them to eBay. You can download the software from the Turbo Lister page.

Turbo Lister is designed for medium- to high-volume sellers. For a comparison of eBay Seller Tools go to the Feature Comparison Table.

With Turbo Lister you can:

- Create professional-looking listings easily using a design editor and templates (no HTML knowledge needed).
- List multiple items all at once.
- Duplicate existing listings and save listings to reuse again and again.
- Change formats or add item specifics to multiple items all at once.
- Access convenient HTML templates.
- Upload thousands of listings to eBay with a single click.
- Add photos and preview your listings without being connected to the Internet.
- Insert in your listings payment terms, tax, shipping and any messages you want to include.
- Import active or completed item listings from eBay to Turbo Lister.
- Edit ore revise active listings on eBay
- Relist and sell similar items on eBay

Contact us

Need help?

[Contact us]

Ask eBay members

Get help from other eBay members Visit the Answer Centre to post a question.

Related Help topics

- Advanced Selling Tools Overview
- Installing Turbo Lister

Selling Manager and Selling Manager Pro

Selling Manager and Selling Manager Pro are both eBay programs. Whereas Turbo Lister is downloaded onto your PC, Selling Manager and Selling Manager Pro are online programs (like Facebook, Google, Gmail, Twitter, eBay, etc.).

The world is moving more and more to online programs (also known as "Cloud-based computing") and away from PC-based software. Cloud-based software has many benefits:

- Automatic, seamless updates.
- Inexpensive rates, as you normally pay a monthly/yearly subscription instead of purchasing an entire product.
- Anyone, anywhere on the planet can use the software, as long as they can connect to the Internet.
- Less expensive hardware. We used to have dedicated mail servers which worked well (until they failed for some reason, or the software crashed). Now we use Google's Gmail, which is cloud-based, and no longer requires an expensive mail server and a dedicated static IP address.

- No software upgrades required.
- Security, as the data is held off-site.

Like most cloud-based software, eBay charges a monthly subscription fee to use Selling Manager Pro (approx $9.95 per month at the time of press) but fees are different in most countries, so please check your eBay site for fees in your location. Selling Manager (at the time of press) is free. Always remember that the point of using new hardware and software is to SAVE MONEY. Many of my students balk when I tell them how much things like Selling Manager Pro cost; then, after they have used it, they come back, telling me how much time and money they have saved since.

Hardware and software are tools, designed to save you time and money. If they are not saving you time and money, then you either have the wrong tool or your business is not large enough (yet) for those tools.

Always do some cost analysis to see if you will save time and money before opening your wallet for a new tool.

Selling Manager features provide the capability to:

- View the status of your listings, and reminders of your next steps, in the "Summary View."
- Manage items to be listed at a future date using "Scheduled View."
- Monitor your active listings using "Active View."
- Manage the items that you have sold using "Sold View."
- Quickly relist items from your "Unsold View."
- View and manage post-sales activities, including feedback, email, payments, and postage.
- Download sales records.
- Complete bulk tasks, including: listing items, relisting your unsold items, leaving feedback, sending email, and printing invoices.

Plus, when you subscribe to Selling Manager, the "All Selling" links in the "My eBay" views are replaced by "Selling Manager" links. This separates all of your eBay listings into "views" to help you manage your scheduled listings, active listings, and post-sales activities.

Selling Manager Pro Features

Selling Manager Pro has all the features of Selling Manager, however, it also has inventory and automation features. These include:

- Viewing "Inventory," "Reporting," and "Automation Preferences."
- Managing products, tracking inventory, and using store listing templates from the Inventory view.
- Viewing and downloading reports about your sales activities.
- Automating certain post-sales tasks, including sending buyers email and leaving feedback.
- Automatically scheduling listings and relisting unsold items.

To see more of the features of Selling Manager and Selling Manager Pro, go to http://pages.eBay.com.au/education/learn-to-sell-tools-comparison.html

How to Subscribe to Selling Manager and Selling Manager Pro

- On any page in eBay, click on "Site Map" (at the bottom of the page).
- Next, click "Selling Manager" or "Selling Manager Pro," located under "Selling Tools."

Site Map

The eBay site is organised into five sections: **Buy, Sell, My eBay, Community** and **Help**. Get an overview of each section below

Buy

Registration
- Confirm Registration
- Register to Buy

Categories
- All Categories
- Alcohol & Food
- Antiques
- Art

Sell

Selling Tools
- eBay Solutions Directory
- eBay Stores
- Sales Reports
- Selling Manager
- Selling Manager Pro
- Turbo Lister

Selling Resources
- PayPal for Sellers

The next step in automation is a big step in your decision process, as now it is time to go with third-party software. Do not go to this stage until you are selling at least 30 items per week.

If you are selling 30 items or more per week, third-party auction management software will save you a ton of time. Among many other functions, this software will: automatically list items on eBay, relist them again when they are sold (if there is more of the same item available), relist items when they don't sell, automatically file unpaid disputes with eBay (so that you get your eBay fees back from customers who purchase items and don't pay for them), print shipping labels, automatically leave feedback for customers, automatically respond to "best offers," automatically send "second chance" offers, etc.

Programs like *Channel Advisor* will even manage your website, and manage your entire inventory.

The three programs that my students use the most are:

- Auctiva (http://www.auctiva.com)
- Channel Advisor (http://channeladvisor.com)
- Auctionsound (http://www.auctionsound.com)

We use Channel Advisor. There are many eBay Listing programs out there, though. To find others, Google "eBay listing software."

The reason this is a big step is that whichever third-party software you decide you need, you must learn that software, and then incorporate your listings into the software.

You really do not want to go to the effort of mastering one piece of software for a few months, then dropping it and moving on to the next, as you will, more than likely, have all your pictures and ad copy hosted by whichever third-party listing software you choose.

When we started looking for eBay listing software, our goal was to become Million Dollar eBay Sellers, so my question at the time was, "What listing software programs do the largest eBay sellers use?"

Back then, in 2006, there were two companies that the most successful eBay sellers used: Marketworks and Channel Advisor. We chose Channel Advisor, or "CA." (Later on, CA bought out Marketworks). Today, CA's customers turn over 35 billion dollars through CA. Don't let me sway you in any direction here, though. CA works well for us, and we are used to it, however there are other eBay listing programs, such as:

- Auctiva (www.auctiva.com)
- Vendio (www.vendio.com)
- Auction Wizard (www.auctionwizard.com)
- Auction Hawk (www.auctionhawk.com)
- Ink Frog (www.inkfrog.com)
- Market Blast (www.marketblast.com)

You can find other listing software at www.solutions.eBay.com

When you are at this stage, make the software vendors work for your business; ask them to demonstrate their software to you. Take your time; this is a big decision, as you will probably stay with whichever software you choose, for a very long time.

(For shipping automation, see Chapter 15).

CHAPTER TWELVE

Strategies and Optimization

"The average human has one breast and one testicle."

~ DES McHALE ~

In the early days of eBay, auctions were the big thing, and the most talked about strategies involved choosing between three-day, seven-day, or ten-day auctions. Today, more items are sold on eBay using Buy it Now (in fact, 98% of our sales are BIN), but auctions can still work for the right products.

Let's first look at auction strategies.

The driver for auctions is the old "Supply and Demand" equation. If you are selling an item, and lots of buyers want one, and there is either little competition OR the competition is selling for higher prices, then you will normally get a good price on auction. This is, again, where buying at a good price becomes very important.

On average (see Chapter 6), auctions that have a 99 cent starting price usually sell for the highest prices because they attract the most watchers, and because buyers' egos kick in at the very end, but this strategy is, of course, risky. The way to reduce the risk is to begin the auction with a starting price. (Do not worry that the higher price will scare the "bargain hunters" away).

If the item cost you, say, $100, then set the starting bid at, say, $110. If you have an expensive item, like a diamond ring, or any other item that has a small audience (due to the price), then setting a starting price is critical.

Auctions require two bidders or more by the end in order to push the price up: preferably, two bidders with big egos, and strong sense of "ownership" for the product they are bidding on!

Be careful of flooding the market with too many auctions at the same time, as it can push the market's "price perception" down. (People mainly see the lowest prices on auctions, due to the inherent way in which an auction works - it only hits the high prices in the last few minutes).

For example: Let's say you are selling a log splitter, and you have listed it with a starting price of 99 cents for a duration of seven days. You start the auction at 9 p.m. on Sunday night, and it finishes seven days later, on the following Sunday night.

At 99 cents, the bids start small, and then gradually go up in price, until the last few minutes when they, very often, rise rapidly.

On Monday, this item might be 99 cents; Tuesday, $10; Wednesday, $20; Thursday, $40; Friday, $40; Saturday, $80; Sunday, $100; and then finally - in the last two minutes of the auction - on Sunday night, at 8:45 p.m., it sells for $160.

During the auction, many people will look at the log splitter, and note the price that the auction is up to, and "perceive" that price as what the splitter is worth (i.e., $40, from Thursday).

As discussed in Chapter 6, the finishing time for auctions is critical, with Sunday night around 9 p.m. being the best for most items; Thursday night, the second best; and Friday night, the worst. Some items work well during the day, with finishing times around

2:30 p.m. Testing or studying previous sales, using the "Completed Listings" button, is the best way to find out the best auction finishing times, as all products and niches are different.

The effect of this low price perception is that if you ALSO have the same item listed with a BIN price of, say, $200, the fact that the same item also has a $40 price on it can put potential buyers off (or, the buyer may wait for the auction to finish).

Whenever you list an item for auction, always include a BIN price, as well as the auction starting price. This helps to set the buyers' perceived price value, and it also allows buyers who don't want to wait until the auction ends to purchase the product immediately. (This type of buyer will snap it up, straight away). If it *does* sell using the BIN option, the auction will end immediately, and you can list another one right away.

Note: When you list an auction with a BIN price as well as an auction starting price, as soon as someone bids on the item, the BIN option is automatically removed by eBay. However, sometimes the auction price will rise higher than the BIN price!

Auction Durations

It does not make a lot of difference whether you list an item for three, five, seven, or ten days: the items seem to sell for damn near the same amount. We have tested this theory literally hundreds, if not thousands of times over the years, however, this is only the case with new items that have a high demand, and if you have multiple of them.

If you are selling anything rare that has a small amount of buyers, or you have a one of a kind product, a 10-day auction is the only way to go. You may as well take as much time as you can to attract as many buyers as possible that would be interested in such a 'one of a kind' item.

The big advantage of choosing 3-day auctions is stock turn. That is, you can sell one item every three days, so you will have three times the amount of turnover than you would with a 10-day auction.

Buy it Now Strategies

Here is a reverse strategy to increase the market's price perception.

Let's say you have 10 log splitters in stock. List the 10 log splitters on a GTC (Good 'Til Cancelled) listing with a high BIN price (e.g., $250) but ALSO with a "Best Offer."

This way, the market's price perception of the item is that it is worth $250, but if a buyer offers, say, $200, and you accept the offer, it is a win-win for both you and the buyer - for buyers because they feel they got a bargain, and for you because you sold the item for $200. HOWEVER, the market's perception is STILL that it is worth $250, as your listing is still displaying $250.

In fact, two good things have now happened to your listing: Your listing now shows "9 available," and significantly, "1 sold."

This is very powerful, for two reasons. Firstly, future buyers see that one has sold, which gives them the warm and fuzzies, and more importantly, eBay's search algorithm takes this sale into account, and can raise your listing higher in the search results. This is called "Sales History," and the eBay algorithm loves sales history, as it proves that the item was relevant to a buyer's search.

Think of this in reverse: If you listed, say, an iPad, and eBay continually showed buyers the listing for your iPad, but no one purchased it (instead, purchasing from other sellers), eBay would eventually stop showing your listing.

Google does exactly the same thing with websites, and it does an amazingly good job at only showing websites which are "relevant to the search." This relevancy has been the secret to why everybody loves eBay and Google. Before Google, I used to use a search engine called "Altavista," and what used to drive me bonkers was when it returned results for a search that was not relevant in any way. I would search for a "new hard drive" for my computer, and Altavista would show me "home loans." What the - !?

Likewise, buyers love eBay, as they can search for something and get a relevant result. Past sales history is a great indicator for the eBay search algorithm that a listing is relevant.

In the screenshot below, this seller has more than 10 available items and has sold 464. The eBay algorithm loves items with sales history:

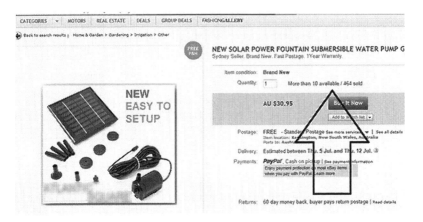

Best Offer

With best offers, eBay will email you the best offers, but you can save time with the auto-decline and auto-accept features in the "Sell Your Item" forum. This automated feature is easy to set up when you create your listing, and will respond to offers immediately by turning down offers that are below your set price or accepting offers that are within your preferred price range.

If you receive offers that are outside of your price settings, you'll need to respond to these offers manually.

Third-party listing software, like Channel Advisor, also looks out for best offers automatically.

As a bonus, there are no eBay listing fees for best offer sales!

Second Chance Offer

If an item sells on auction for say, $50, and you are happy with any amount over, say, $40, eBay allows you to send a "Second Chance Offer" to any bidders who bid over $40. This is a terrific way of getting more sales when an auction sells for a high price, and an added bonus is that with every "second chance" sale you get, you pay no listing fees.

To send a Second Chance Offer:

1. Go to "My eBay."
2. Click the "Sold" or "Unsold" link.
3. Find the item.
4. From the "Actions" drop-down menu next to the item, select "Second Chance Offer."
5. Click the "Continue" button.
6. Select the quantity of items you have to sell, the duration of the offer, and the bidders you want to send offers to.
7. Click the "Continue" button.

The number of offers you can send depends on the quantity of duplicate items you select to offer. For example, if you have four duplicate items, you can send offers to up to four bidders. You'll also receive a copy of the offer email that was sent to bidders.

Markdown Manager

Markdown Manager is used to create sales for both the auction-style and Fixed Price (Buy It Now) listings in your store.

You can create themed sales for seasons, specific holidays, different, specific categories, or simply to clear out your inventory.

Whenever you have a sale, eBay automatically displays the little gold circle with the discount symbol inside, as per the picture below:

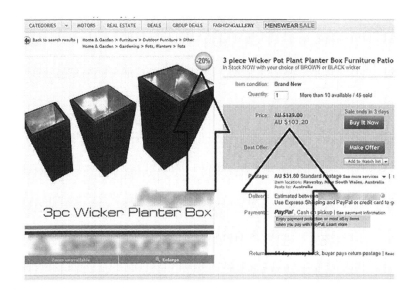

Determining Discounts

You can choose to offer a price discount or a free postage discount. If you select free postage on any of your listings, eBay automatically shows the orange "Free Postage" icon on your listing(s).

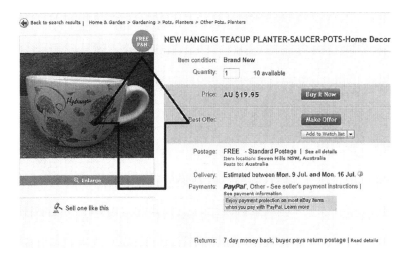

Fixed Price (Buy It Now) listings can be discounted by a percentage amount (from 5% to 75%), or by a specific monetary amount (e.g., "$10 off"). For example, if an item is currently selling for $100, it can be discounted by 10% or, alternatively, by $10. This means that the item is on sale for $90, in both cases.

Discounts can't be applied to auction-style listings, but you can select a free postage discount for any listing, including Fixed Price (Buy It Now) and auction-style listings, as long as they have been listed for seven days prior. Markdown Manager will not work with any listings that have not been listed for at least seven days.

To create sales in Markdown Manager:

1. Go to "My eBay."
2. From the Account tab, select "Marketing Tools."

3. Click "Markdown Manager" on the left side of the page.

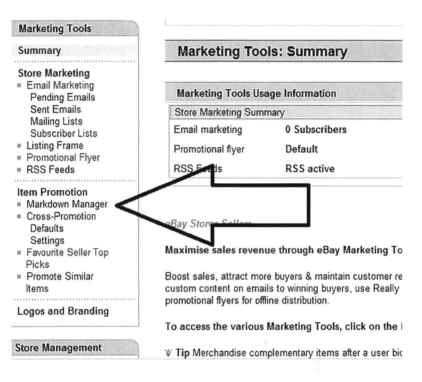

4. Next, click the "Create Sale" button.
5. Once a sale is created, you'll receive a "success" message. If you schedule more than 200 listings in your sale, you'll receive an email to let you know when your sale is created.

We normally run 10% off sales once per month.

eBay Listing Analytics

eBay's Listing Analytics is, at the time of writing, a free subscription from eBay. Listing Analytics allows you to see how your listings are performing by comparing them to other listings, based on the keywords you enter.

For example, let's say you are selling hydraulic log splitters. Within Listing Analytics, you can search for "hydraulic log splitter," and it will show you the following information:

- **Current Rank** - The position of your listing when a buyer searches for a keyword(s) (i.e., "hydraulic," "log," "splitter"). Obviously, ranking in the Top 20 is better than ranking 300. In the screenshot below, you can see the top 4 ranked listing for this search:

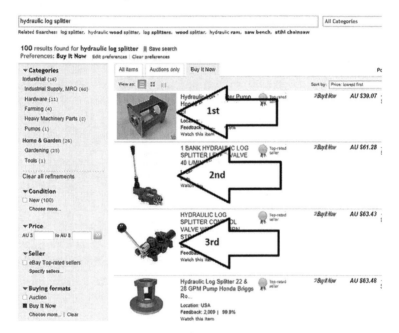

- **Title** - The 80 characters you used when listing the item.
- **Format** - Auction or BIN.
- **Impressions** - The number of times eBay has displayed your listing. This does not mean how many times someone has clicked on your listing; just how many times it has been displayed in search results.

- **Clicks** - The number of times a buyer has clicked on your listing.
- **Click Through** - This is shown as a percentage, based on impressions/clicks.
- **Sold Items** - The number of times buyers have purchased an item from your listing. This number will only be greater than one when your listing is a multiple quantity, fixed price listing.
- **Sell through** - The number of items that sold divided by the number of clicks for your listing. The higher the sell through rate, the better, meaning that members were more likely to buy your item when they clicked to view your listing.
- **Watchers** - The total number of members watching your listing.
- **Sales** - Total dollar amount sold: Sold items x sales price.
- **Revise** - This is where you can make on-the-fly, instant changes to your listing.

The great thing you can do with this information is sort by columns (i.e., sort by rank to find out which of your listings are the best and worst performers). Then you can compare the worst performers to the competition to see what you are doing differently. You can then make on-the-fly revisions to your listing(s). By the time you return, say, one week later, you can check again to see how your modifications changed the ranking.

By continually "tuning up your listings," you can stay on top of the competition.

Subscribing to Listing Analytics

Listing Analytics (at the time of writing) is free. Here's how to subscribe:

1. Go to "My eBay."
2. Click the "Applications" tab.
3. Click the "Go to the Apps Center" link.
4. Look for "Listing Analytics."
5. Click the "Subscribe" button.

After you've subscribed, you can use Listing Analytics any time by going to the "Applications" tab in "My eBay."

Sales Reports

eBay offers a very good reporting tool called "Sales Reports," and the more feature-rich "Sales Reports Plus." Sales Reports is a free subscription, and Sales Reports Plus is $6.99, however, it comes with a free, 30-day trial.

Sales Reports gives you the following information:

- Total sales.
- Ended listings.
- Average sale price.
- eBay and PayPal fees.

Sales Reports Plus gives you the following information:

- Metrics by category.
- Metrics by format (e.g., Fixed Price).
- Metrics by category and format.
- Metrics by day or time for all formats.
- Buyer counts.
- Detailed eBay fees.

- Unpaid Item Credits requested.
- Ability to show or hide sections.
- Download capabilities.

To subscribe to Sales Reports, go to "Site Map" (at the bottom of every eBay page). Then, from the middle column, click on "Sales Reports." Once you have subscribed, click on "My eBay," and then select "Sales Reports" from the Account tab.

Auction Sniper

Auction sniper is not a selling strategy, however, it deserves a mention due to the effect it has on auctions.

Auction sniper and other sniping programs are designed to win auctions at the lowest possible price by bidding in the last few seconds of an auction (usually five seconds before an auction ends).

If you stop and think about auctions, it makes no sense to bid on an auction at any time except during the last few seconds from the end of the auction. If you do bid earlier, all you do is push the price up, and then the next bidder pushes the price up even further. The smart thing to do at any auction, whether it is buying a $5 iPad case on eBay or a one million dollar piece of real estate, is to do absolutely NOTHING till the absolute last, possible second.

If I am buying real estate at a real estate auction, I wait until the hammer is already falling and literally just about to hit the table before shouting my hopefully one-and-only killer bid. Before that bid, no one in the room knew I existed, and the last bidder who really thought he or she had won the auction is usually dumbfounded and bewildered by my out-of-nowhere bid. I have won many auctions this way.

Very similar with eBay: If you enter your one-and-only *killer* bid in the last few seconds, all other bidders will not have a chance to outbid you. This, of course, is a good buying strategy, but as sellers, we need lots of bidders with big egos!

The reason I bring this up is because some markets have smarter bidders than others. Computer-savvy people are getting more and more knowledgeable about programs like Auction Sniper, and thus making auctions less profitable.

This is another reason why BIN is more popular today than auctions.

eBay Optimization

The secret to a highly profitable eBay business is to have many high-profit items.

To do this, we occasionally need to tweak some existing ad copy or quickly get rid of any slow-selling items.

A slow item is a lost profit opportunity. That is, the money and storage space for a slow item needs to be converted to a fast-selling, high-profit item. What is a slow seller? Any item which, on average, has a sell frequency of less than one per week.

Everybody gets a slow item at some stage, and it is important to recognize a slow item quickly in order to take action to move it. I will show you some of the strategies we use.

First, check the basics by comparing your listing to other sellers' listings, according to the following criteria:

1) Price. If auction, what is their start price? Do you or they have a reserve? Buy it Now? How does your price compare to the competition?

2) Top Rated seller. What is different about your listing compared with the Top-rated sellers' listings?

3) Title: Are you using similar keywords in the 80-character title? Keywords are critical. Every good keyword brings more traffic to your listing. eBay allows us 80 characters: try to use all 80 characters. The title is the only place in which the eBay search engine looks for basic searches. Keywords

elsewhere, like in the body of the listing, will not help you unless a buyer does an advanced search.

4) Bullet points: Do you have lots of bullet points, with features and benefits? Have you converted the features to benefits? The idea here is to create a "high perceived value" of your item by pointing out every single feature and benefit you can find, and then listing them in multiple bullet points. If it's got it, list it in a bullet point!

5) Pictures. Make sure your pictures are clear, detailed and on a white background. Like bullet points, show every benefit and feature in your pictures to create a "high perceived value."

6) How many feedbacks do you have? If less than 10, then you should work to get your ratings up by either selling unused items from around the house, or second-hand items from places like garage sales. This is what we did to gain experience when we got started, and it got our feedback well over 10, while providing a lot of lessons along the way.

7) Shipping. eBay encourages sellers to offer free shipping, and they will show your listing more often if you have free shipping. eBay even puts an orange circle with the words "Free Shipping" on your listing, automatically.

We have conducted many tests for charged shipping versus free shipping, and free shipping outsells almost every time. If you sell an item for $10 with $5 shipping and/or the same item for $15 with free shipping, the one with the free shipping will be the winner.

eBay's Secret Weapon: "Markdown Manager."

If you have completed all of the steps above and your item is still slow, then it is time to bring out the big gun: eBay's Markdown Manager.

Markdown Manager allows you to easily, consistently drop the price until you hit the sweet spot, and displays the discount to your customers as a percentage off. Always list the item with a high price so that the discount seems bigger to the customer. Again: "perceived value."

For a slow item or an item we want to move, we run weekly sales, with the 1st sale at 10% off. On the second week, 15% (etc.), until we hit the sweet spot.

Every item has a price that will make it more competitive.

Note: Markdown manager can only be used for listings which are over seven days old. It will not work for new listings.

Record Keeping

Start your record keeping when you are beginning your business as this is much easier than if you put it off for a year. There are tons of computer bookkeeping programs out there, but the most popular record-keeping software for eBay sellers is QuickBooks. QuickBooks is, of course, available for purchase on eBay.

eBay and most third-party auction management software programs have data feeds which can be uploaded straight into QuickBooks.

You can learn QuickBooks by either purchasing a book like *QuickBooks for Dummies* or attending a short, part-time night course at a local school or community college.

The added bonus of using a program like QuickBooks is that you can easily produce reports to see exactly how much money you are making, and in the early days, to find out exactly when your home business makes more money than you can make working for somebody else.

I cannot over-emphasize how important it is to be able to print off a report once a month and see your total sales, and exactly how much the stock cost for those sales.

By seeing exactly how much profit you are making on a monthly basis, you can figure out when to add more staff (like a bookkeeper), which in turn gives you more time for the other things you like to do in life, like celebrating holidays (etc.).

For most people, the idea of learning a bookkeeping/account-ing program like QuickBooks scares them to death, but there is no need to be scared. Today, with the use of modern GUI (Graphic User Interface), QuickBooks (like all modern software) is simple to learn and user-friendly. You don't need to know all of its func-tions - far from it - just learn enough to be able to produce the basic reports (like a profit and loss statement and a balance sheet). Your job is not to become an accountant! Just be knowledgeable enough to be able to produce basic reports.

The great thing with QuickBooks is that it is the most-used bookkeeping software for eBay sellers on the planet, and there are thousands of certified QuickBooks bookkeepers. So if you get stuck, just go to the QuickBooks website and look through the "Certified Advisor" database for a QuickBooks bookkeeper in your area.

Most accountants these days can use your QuickBooks data file to quickly produce your end-of-year tax returns. If your accountant does not know how to use QuickBooks, then it really is time to find a new accountant.

To speed things up, ask whichever bank you are using to switch you from paper statements to electronic. This way, your bank state-ments will be emailed to you monthly, and you can just save them to a folder on your computer. Then, when your accountant asks for your bank statements and your QuickBooks data file, you can sim-ply and quickly email all the information without having to scan or photocopy any statements.

Exit Strategy

One of the first things you need to plan when you start any business is your exit strategy out of the business. An eBay business is a very saleable business: in fact, it is one of the most saleable businesses out there. eBay businesses demand top prices, of one to four times the profit the business makes in one year, plus inventory.

For instance, let's say an eBay business makes a profit of $500,000 per annum. This business can be sold from $500,000 to $2,000,000, plus the cost of any stock. The 1-4 ratio depends on factors such as how well the business can run without you, how diverse the product range is so that it can weather any storm, and how long the business has been running. Basically, the buyer wants to make sure they not only get their money back from the purchase, but also makes a good profit over time.

While you own an eBay business, it is a terrific cash-generating machine, returning profits every day.

When you sell it, it is a great *capital asset*, in that you can use the capital for your nest egg.

The exit strategy can be used once for retirement, or as a continuous strategy to build up small eBay businesses from scratch and then sell them.

There is a huge market for home businesses due to the people who have recently left the workforce and are all cashed up from their superannuation/401K funds. These people do not want to start a business from scratch: their background is normally corporate, and they are used to following set procedures in business, which is why they like to buy expensive franchises.

To accommodate these potential buyers, create a procedures manual with lots of screenshots showing exactly what you do every day. It is not hard to create a procedures manual - the last one I did took me less than one day to complete.

You may choose not to sell the business, but instead keep it as a cash machine for your retirement, or even pass it on to your children.

CHAPTER THIRTEEN

Storage

"*Don't be afraid to give your best to what seemingly are small jobs. Every time you conquer one it makes you that much stronger. If you do the little jobs well, the big ones will tend to take care of themselves.*"

~ DALE CARNEGIE ~

Where to store inventory is a question I get asked a lot, so I thought it would be best to write a chapter on all the different options we use or have used.

Obviously, the best place to store inventory for a home business is at your house, but if you have a one bedroom studio apartment, then it does not take long before your studio looks like a small warehouse, and even the cat is having a hard time finding somewhere to sleep!

Consider every square meter of your property, as it is either reserved for living space or for your business. If it has been reserved for business use, then that square meter must earn its keep and make a profit. In Sydney, storage at a self-storage company costs approx $11 per cubic meter, per month.

Always make your storage space pay for itself. If an item is collecting dust and not making money, in a space allocated for business, either sell it off cheaply or dump it.

If you allocate a one square meter area, also pack it to the roof by using storage racks. As simple as this sounds, many people forget to store to the roof with racks, and go out searching for more space, too soon. Storage space costs money, so maximize on what you have first.

When we import containers from China, our rule is: "We do not want to import any Chinese air." By that, we mean we want every nook and cranny in the container filled. The more items you fit in a container, the cheaper the shipping is, as the fixed shipping price can be divided by more items.

Same with storage: You want to fit the absolute most in each square meter. The picture below is a typical, assemble-yourself shelf. This style of shelving is available from all major home improvement stores. Try to get the highest and deepest ones to maximize storage.

If you own a house, then obviously your options for storage are greater. We use the 80/20 principal to maximize usable space: i.e., if an item gets rarely used, it gets fed up through the manhole into our roof cavity. (This is the part of the roof in between the tiles and the roof, a.k.a., an attic). Below is a picture of an empty roof cavity.

You don't have to put down a fancy floor; you can just get some old, used pieces of timber and place them over the rafters.

The next piece of space utilization is the garage (if you have one): Again, use the 80/20 principal to work out what gets used and what doesn't. Remove any unused items and either sell them off, put them in the roof cavity, or move them to a garden shed (if you have one).

If you don't have a garden shed and you need more storage space, consider it. Garden sheds come in all different shapes and sizes.

With garage and garden shed storage, if there is any chance at all that water may leak onto the floor, you must create a simple, false floor to eliminate the risk of your inventory being destroyed by water damage. I even dug a hole in the lowest spot in one garage, and installed a drain with an electric water pump and float switch, just in case! It has never been required, but it is better to be safe than sorry!

False floors can be created using lengths of cheap timber or bricks lying on the ground, and then laying cheap timber on top. Most modern homes these days use a water-resistant particle board flooring. This is perfect, as it is cheap and easy to work with. In Australia, they call it "yellow tongue" as it has a piece of yellow plastic (tongue) on one side, which slots into the groove on the other side.

Yellow tongue, tongue and groove, water-resistant particle board flooring.
The next area we used to store stock was an upstairs, outdoor patio. For this, we enclosed the patio with tinted "bistro blinds."

These PVC blinds zip together, making them waterproof, and are easy to hang up. We used the smoked charcoal color as opposed to the clear blinds, and then hung shade cloth behind so the inventory was not visible to neighbors (etc.). Patio/café/bistro blinds and shade cloth are available from most home improvement stores.

Before we move on to paid storage, there are two more options, if you have the room. The first is to purchase an old shipping container:

I have purchased these for $1,000 in Australia on eBay, and they make for terrific waterproof storage facilities. I purchased the first one, sight-unseen, and later discovered the roof was rusted out. We fixed it by painting the roof with bitumen, but check the roof first before handing over your money.

The next thing we did as we grew was purchase an old Pantech truck which used to be a removalist (moving) truck. (This old truck ran okay, but it had already travelled 925,000 kilometers by the time of purchase). Whereas a container can store approximately 30 cubic meters, the old truck could hold 40 cubic meters, and as a bonus, we had a truck to take things like cardboard to the recycling center.

Some of my coaching clients in America purchased old, unregistered motor homes, then gutted them inside; others purchased old caravans and did the same. One of them who purchased an old, ugly, yellow caravan painted it green just by using a paintbrush, then grew a vine over it so it was nearly invisible in the yard! If you have the space, do the math to see how much it will cost you to purchase something like an old caravan, compared to paying for storage.

Don't forget, you can always sell it later on, whereas you cannot get back money from paying for storage.

Don't let me put you off paying for storage, though. Just remember that storage should ALWAYS pay for itself.

For example, if you are storing, say, one cubic meter of a chic, fancy dress outfit, and you sell 30 of these per month at a $17 profit each, this is $510 gross profit, minus the storage of, say, $15 for the cubic meter of storage for the month: Net profit, $495.

Once you have run out of storage space at home and you need more storage for inventory, you have the option of paying for storage or using a fulfillment house. A fulfillment house will hold your stock and ship it for you to your customers.

All you need to do with a fulfillment house is send them the details, every morning, of which items you want posted, and they will package and mail them out for you. Many fulfillment houses have very smart software, and you can simply upload a spreadsheet file to their software every morning.

Fulfillment houses work great but they obviously cost money. To find a fulfillment house in your country, Google "fulfillment services."

Personally, I like to have my inventory close to me so I am able to touch and see it – plus, the extra profit is always nice.

I have been to many seminars where speakers from fulfillment houses stand on stage, claiming they can ship cheaper than most small eBay sellers can, as they get better rates from shipping carriers due to the mass amount they ship. I have never found this to be the case. Yes, they do get good rates, but they do not sell the shipping to you at cost price. Most fulfillment houses make money on shipping.

Once you are shipping more than 30 items per week, talk to whichever shipping carrier you are using and ask for a commercial rate.

Rent an Unused Car Garage

There are many people who live in houses and apartments who do not use their lockup garage. You can find these being advertised in local newspapers, or you can be pro-active and create a mailer which you can drop into people's letter boxes.

Self Storage

Self storage centers seem to popping up everywhere (or is it just that I am noticing them all the time now?). A self storage center is often an open building which a business has converted into many lockup storage areas.

Self storage units have the advantage of scalability. That is, you normally only have to give one month's notice so you can upscale to more storage units, and scale down to less storage units, depending on how much inventory you are holding. The other advantage over renting someone else's car garage is that self-storage sites normally have 24/7 video surveillance.

When you get to the stage of importing whole containers, the storage units work well, as there is normally plenty of space to unload a container, which is on the back of a truck while the truck waits. It normally takes around 45 minutes for 3 people to unload a 20-foot container.

CHAPTER 14

Postage and Packing

Every country has different options for shipping, but the concept is always the same, which is to get goods packed as fast and as inexpensively as possible, and to ensure that deliveries arrive in one piece.

"Slapping" is what can cause a ton of damage (i.e., if you put a small item in a large box with no padding, and then tip the box on its end, the item will slide down and "slap" the bottom).

Slapping should be avoided by filling large boxes with some kind of packing material, like rolled-up old newspapers (heavy) or bags of foam peanuts (which you can purchase from a packaging company).

If you are new or on a budget, you can get used packing boxes for free from local shops who throw them out. You can also make your own padding by scrunching up old newspapers.

When we started out, we got ourselves a fold-out table, a big roll of brown paper, a tape gun and a set of digital scales. Depending on the size of the items you sell, you may also need:

- Mailing tubes
- Boxes
- Bubble wrap
- Labels

Some companies, like USPS, can provide labels which work with thermal printers. If you use these, you will need a thermal printer, but the great thing about thermal printers is they do not require any toner or ink to work.

Roll of brown paper

Tape Gun

We purchased the table from a local home improvement store, the tape gun and brown paper from a local packaging company, and digital scales from eBay. The scales go up to 25 kg (approx. 50 lbs) and cost less than $50.

Today, we prefer using boxes to hand-wrapping items in brown paper, as we found the time it took to pay someone to wrap an item by hand cost more than purchasing a custom-made cardboard box. When you get to this stage, use a stopwatch to time how long it takes to hand-wrap an item with paper, then divide that time into the hourly rate you pay the person.

Once you have calculated how much it costs in labor, contact a cardboard box manufacturer to get some quotes for boxes.

Labels

Many people, when they start an eBay business, hand-write the name and address on the parcel they are sending, and this is fraught with danger. Unless you have brilliant handwriting, the address can very often be misread somewhere along the postal system or worse still, get lost, or delivered to someone else. If you do write by hand, over time, almost everybody will make some kind of writing error which will cause a problem.

The simplest method at the beginning is to print out the email you receive from eBay when an item is sold, then cut the name and address out with scissors. You can then quickly tape this onto the parcel. This way, the name and address is crystal clear, and there are no accidental mistakes (like leaving off a number of the address).

If you live in the U.S., you can print labels (even UPS labels) straight from your PayPal account.

To do this, click the "Ship" button, which is to the right of every payment in the "Overview" page of your PayPal account.

At the time of writing, this feature was available to PayPal USA customers only.

Later on, when you use auction management software, the software will print the labels for you.

Shipworks

Shipworks (http://www.shipworks.com) connects to eBay, automatically imports your sales information from eBay, and then automatically exports that information into shipping carriers such as Fedex, UPS, etc. This saves a ton of time. Unfortunately, at the time of writing, Shipworks is only available in the U.S., but they have assured me they are going to be expanding into other countries, so you may want to send them an email.

Epilogue

We started selling on eBay as it met many of the criteria we wanted for a home business. We wanted a business where we could work from home and spend more time with our children.

The more time we spent with eBay, the more we realized just how big eBay is in the world. Today, there are over 100 million active eBay users. Never before have we all been blessed with such a huge work-from-home opportunity; never before have we had access to over 7 billion computer users – worldwide - from our comfortable couches in our living rooms.

The world has changed. Every month, more shoppers switch their buying habits to eBay, and fewer shoppers are driving to their local mall. Yesterday, I required a 4.2 mm drill bit for a project I am working on. My options were to drive 15 minutes each way to the store, or find it on eBay. Yep, I chose eBay, and there it was, for $2, including free postage to my front door. I saved myself half an hour, purchased what I wanted, and almost certainly got it cheaper than what I would have paid at a traditional bricks and mortar store where the store owner has huge overheads like rent, staff to chat with, customers, and royalties to pay to the mall.

This what is happening in the world: it is simply more convenient to purchase on eBay, and the human race always follows the path of least resistance. When it comes to products, there is more variety, and they're cheaper, too.

This switchover by the public, from shopping at bricks and mortar stores to making purchases online, offers work-from-home entrepreneurs an enormous opportunity to supply this relatively new, but incredibly enormous, worldwide market, while enjoying all the comfort - and tax advantages - of working from home.

Working from home has never, ever been easier. Unlike almost all other businesses, you can start an eBay business with absolutely no money, and pay no rent for an office or its design.

From your living room, you have access to unlimited amounts of new products, and you do not even have to cold-call any customers! You can build a small, part-time eBay business, or a giant Titanium business - the choice is yours.

Without a doubt, eBay is the most exciting business we have ever been involved in. We have had the great pleasure of helping and witnessing hundreds of our students change their lives by increasing their incomes via their new eBay businesses.

I urge everybody to at least build a part-time eBay business to generate some extra income, and if they have fun doing it, then turn the throttle up and go full-time!

Good luck and I hope to meet you at the next eBay seminar.

Neil Waterhouse

neil@neilwaterhouse.com

Index

74081202R10141

Made in the USA
Columbia, SC
25 July 2017